POLAND
SOLIDARITY
WALESA

POLAND : SOLIDAR

SOLIDARNOŚĆ
TY:WALESA

MICHAEL DOBBS

K. S. KAROL

DESSA TREVISAN

McGRAW-HILL BOOK COMPANY

NEW YORK   SAN FRANCISCO   ST. LOUIS

A McGraw-Hill Co-Publication

Copyright © 1981 by McGraw-Hill
Book Company (UK) Limited, Maidenhead,
England. All rights reserved. Except as permitted
under the Copyright Act of 1976, no part of this
publication may be reproduced, or distributed in any
form or by any means, or stored in a data base or
retrieval system, without the prior written permission of the publisher.

Library of Congress Cataloging in Publication Data
Dobbs, Michael, 1950-
    Poland/Solidarity/Walesa.
    Includes index.
    1. NSZZ "Solidarność" (Labor Organization)
2. Walesa, Lech, 1943-. Trade-unions—Poland—
Political activity. I. Trevisan, Dessa. II. Karol, K.S.
III. Title.
HD8537.N783D6   331.88'09438   81-6063
ISBN 0-07-006681-7   AACR2

Designer:
CHARLES WHITEHOUSE

Editor:
DAVID BAKER

Managing Editor:
FRANCINE PEETERS

Production Manager:
FRANZ GISLER

Translator (text of K.S. Karol):
ALISON MARTIN

Picture captions by McGRAW-HILL STAFF

Composition by:
FEBEL A.G., BASEL, SWITZERLAND

Photolithography by:
COLOR PART: ACTUAL, BIEL, SWITZERLAND
BLACK AND WHITE: BUSAG GRAPHIC A.G., BERN,
SWITZERLAND

Printed and bound by RICHARD CLAY

Printed in Great Britain

CONTENTS

DESSA TREVISAN
Why Poland? Background to Crisis 10

*Influence of Polish-Soviet relations—origins of the Pol-
ish kingdom—the partitions—Polish nationalism—re-
establishment of Poland—Polish-Soviet War—anti-
sovietism—World War II—resistance—rebirth of the
Polish Communist Party—the Communists take
power—Stalinism and Russian control—the 1956
riots—a cultural renaissance—disappointed expectations—Edward Gierek and "dynamic growth"—the
Church in Poland*

K.S. KAROL
The Peaceful Revolution 48

*A new movement in Eastern Europe—the first strikes—
Western reaction—shortcomings of the Gierek regime—
the police and public reaction—the Party's attitude
to the strikes—the Gdansk Agreement and the fall of
Gierek—revolutionary innovations—Solidarity—the
intellectuals' involvement—struggle within the Party—provocation of Solidarity—restructuring the Party
—economic problems—the relationship with Russia*

MICHAEL DOBBS
Lech Walesa:
Symbol of the Polish August 86

*Walesa as a revolutionary symbol—his rise to promi-
nence—meeting Walesa in Gdansk—the principle of
solidarity—Walesa's childhood and youth—move to
Gdansk and marriage—the lessons of 1970–1976—
the "Baltic committee"—consequences for Walesa—
the "Polish August"—his style of leadership—problems
of celebrity—Walesa and the Church—crisis: Bielsko-
Biala and Bydgoszcz—Walesa's achievement*

PICTURE CREDITS 126

INDEX 127

LECH WALESA
IN THE WORLD ARENA

One day he was an unknown, unemployed, blacklisted electrician, a thirty-seven-year-old father of six who had stood up to Polish authorities and seemed to have been permanently defeated. The next day, he emerged as leader of a new, independent labor organization— Solidarity—with millions of members. Since

August 1980 the man and his followers have astonished the whole world. By June 1981, tensions in Poland seemed to have eased, and the threat of Soviet intervention had apparently passed. There was time for a visit to Geneva, where Walesa addressed the worldwide International Labor Organization to tremendous acclaim. Why had he come? "We want to show the world that we exist." Delegates to the conference from more than a hundred nations stood in line to shake his hand or get an autograph.

But there was no applause, and no handshake, from the Soviet delegation. The Party leadership in Moscow, at that very moment, was sending Polish leaders an ulitimatum "...if Poland is not defended by the Socialist states, then the greedy hand of Imperialism would reach out to seize this country." All of Solidarity's gains now hung in the balance.

7

A YEAR OF CRISIS

The events of 1980–1981 in Poland have been without precedent. No other Socialist republic in the world has ever agreed to negotiate with an unofficial trade union, or even recognized the right of such an organization to exist. Their right to strike has also been given official, if grudging, recognition, and a whole series of

daring demands have been met. Throughout this extraordinary year the images of change and renewal sprang up on every side. Solidarity posters (top picture)—which would have been rigorously banned just a year ago—are now plastered over every available wall space in Polish cities. Solidarity called warning strikes of a few hours' duration, such as this one (above) at Warsaw's Huta Warszawa plant. Mass was even said inside the steel mill at Nowa Huta during one of these two-hour work stoppages (right).

Negotiating as equals (left): *The feisty little electrician in an official tête-à-tête with a chief of state, Walesa being received by General Wojciech Jaruzelski, head of the Polish government. By his time (February 1981) Walesa was throwing all his weight behind the government's effort to maintain the peace and keep Moscow from becoming alarmed. The labor leader was now showing signs of statesmanship and far-sightedness.*

Tense moments for Poland's government and Party leaders. Cabinet minister Stefan Olszowski, chief of state Jaruzelski, with the poster of Lenin behind him, and Communist party chairman Stanislaw Kania show many signs of concern, during a Party plenum in June 1981. Preparations were under way for the Polish Party Congress scheduled to convene in July. From Poland's neighbors in the Warsaw Pact alliance, warnings and threats were becoming more frequent. "Hardliners" in the Polish Party voiced their anger and frustration at the past year's "counterrevolutionary" tide, as if asking the Soviet Union to intervene. The eleven-member Polish Communist Politburo, the top leadership of the Party, confirmed their commitment to renewal and democratization—a note confirmed by Party chief Kania in his response to Soviet warnings. Another crisis was building. Western officials and newspaper editorials called upon the U.S.S.R. to "let Poland be Poland." And the historic Party Congress convened without impediment.

9

DESSA TREVISAN

Why Poland? Background to Crisis

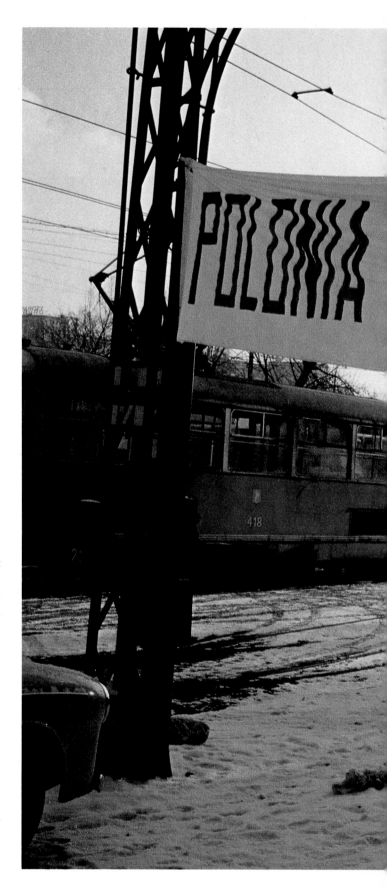

Poland's history and her past are very much part of the landscape, part of the present-day climate. In few countries of Europe do historical and geopolitical factors play such an important role in the settlement of social conflicts and national dilemmas.

In their current search for new solutions, young Poles, knowingly or unknowingly, are breaking the chains which tie them to tradition and force them to endure the torments of unfortunate historical experiences.

Events in 1980–1981 have awakened the feeling of protest and of genuine national consciousness. The variety of political and social ideas that have suddenly come to life have offered the Poles the opportunity of an open confrontation with rightist and leftist dogmas. But basic

"Poland ever faithful." The old Polish Catholic motto, transformed into a modern banner of protest, hangs on the strikebound Warsaw tram depot in January 1981.

political ideology still remains closed to criticism, and ideological pluralism is still only an illusion.

Basically, Poland is conditioned by three historical factors which no one disputes, and which, for a long time to come, cannot be subject to any serious revision:

1. The political, historical, and geographic foundation of Polish-Soviet relations.
2. A pluralism of ideological outlook, whereby the two most influential schools of thought, the Marxist and the Roman Catholic, exist side by side without engaging in a dialogue.
3. Control and direct influence from "outside factors"— the Soviet Communist party domination of political evolution and transformations within the Communist party of Poland.

These three elements constitute the framework in which

social, economic, and political conditions have developed in past decades.

In the course of the past two centuries Poland was three times partitioned by her mighty neighbors, Russia, Prussia, and Austria-Hungary; her territory decreased and was eventually erased from the map. The consequences are still felt today, for the present frontiers of Poland have not yet been fully absorbed in the national consciousness.

Encroachments by her German and Russian neighbors had begun much earlier—almost as far back as Polish history can be traced. It was in fact a German warrior who "discovered" Poland, and left us the first historical record of the existence of a Polish state (a small principate around Gniezno) in the year 963. Its leader, Prince Mieszko, became a Christian in 966 as part of his program of westernization. He found that the only safeguard against German invaders was to form an association with them, and thus his state became a dependency of the Holy Roman (German) Empire under Otto I. For good measure, Mieszko paid homage to the Pope and recognized the authority of the Holy See over all his lands. The integration into Western Europe, however, did not protect him from his Russian neighbor—Vladimir the Great seized an eastern Polish province—and conflicts with bordering states were to remain a constant of Polish history.

The Piast kingdom (992–1384), though it included some truly outstanding rulers, continued to fall prey to invasions, including that of the Mongols in 1241. Some provinces such as Pomerania (the seacoast) changed hands several times, and for nearly two centuries (1138–1314) Poland remained divided among the heirs of Boleslaw III. A turning point came under Wladyslaw I (1314–1333), whose military conquests led to a reunification and expansion of the Polish kingdom. Though Russia and the German states remained a threat, Poland held onto her independence thanks to alliances with Hungary (during the reign of Casimir III the Great, 1333–1370) and later Lithuania (the Jagiellon dynasty, 1386–1572).

An altogether striking aspect of Poland's early political development was the rise of a system of representative councils or diets *(Sejm, plural Sejmiki),* which grew from modest local bodies into a congress which deliberated on a national scale. The first full-fledged *Sejm* was convened in Piotrkow in 1493, and by 1550 the parliamentary system, based on two houses of the *Sejm,* was an established

The resistance leader Tadeusz Kosciuszko, whose extraordinary life included service as a volunteer adviser in the American Revolution of 1776, for which he was given American citizenship. He returned to his native Poland on two occasions to lead uprisings against the Russian occupation including the short-lived triumph of 1794. He is one of Poland's most honored patriots.

fact. The lack of an heir to succeed King Sigismund II in 1572 led to the first election of a monarch in Poland, at the Warsaw *Sejm* on 11 May 1573. Poland and England were thus the only parliamentary states in a Europe otherwise given over to absolutist rule, and most of Poland's rulers between 1573 and 1764 were elected, while the *Sejm* continued to assemble every two years.

The independence of Poland's lesser nobility, in fact, is considered by some historians to have drained the nation's strength at a time, in the late sixteenth and early seventeenth century, when the Poles might otherwise have gained the advantage over Germany and Russia. There were in fact military victories over Russia (1610–1611, 1618, 1634), during Poland's wars of territorial expansion, but the Russians struck back in a crushing invasion while Sweden also occupied extensive Polish territory. An outburst of civil strife in 1664 made it all the easier for Moscow to impose unfavorable terms on Poland in the truce of Andruszow (1667); and Poland's fortunes continued to decline for most of the next hundred years. Already, during the Northern War (1700–1721), Sweden, Saxony, and Russia had plundered Poland at will and Augustus II, the country's Saxon ruler, proposed that most of Poland be divided up between Austria, Prussia, and Russia. Fifty years later, in 1772, this partition

became a reality, and in two subsequent partitions the powers progressively increased their shares until Poland by 1795 officially ceased to exist.

If the first partition had been motivated purely by the great powers' ambitions, the second and third were, partially at least, responses to Polish liberation movements. The second partition (1793) followed Russian suppression of an uprising led by Prince Jozef Poniatowski and Tadeusz Kosciuszko. Kosciuszko, leading a peasant army and proclaiming himself dictator, returned to win major victories over the Russians, and recaptured Warsaw and other territories in 1794 before Russia succeeded in turning the tide. He was captured and Warsaw suffered a bloodbath at Russian hands—as it would later against the Germans in 1944. Russia now took the lion's share of the remaining Polish territory, eradicating the Polish state.

*The maps show Poland's progressive disappearance
from the map of Europe in the course of the three partitions: 1772, 1793, 1795. The colors indicate the territory taken each time by Prussia (blue), Austria-
Hungary (green), and Russia (red). Despite repeated
insurrections Poland was not liberated and reunited
until the end of World War I.*

Polish patriots cast their lot with France in an effort to free their fatherland, but always in vain. French revolutionary leaders failed to help Kosciuszko in 1794, and though Napoleon rewarded the hard-fighting Polish soldiers in his Grand Army by restoring part of Poland as "the Duchy of Warsaw," the Russians recouped the territory following his defeat. Poland was not to be freed until 1918.

Disappointment in Napoleon, rebellions against Czarist Russia, the cult of Kosciuszko, resistance to Germanization, and faith in the great rebirth of the Polish nation, of its statehood and culture: all this has been accumulating for generations, creating in Europe the Polish stereotype of eccentric people, of great individualism, and great courage. Their participation in liberation movements and battles of other nations, under the well-known Polish slogan "for your freedom and our own" (the first of these heroic commitments had been the Poles' rescue of Vienna against the Turks in 1683), won them the reputation of good and fearless soldiers.

At the beginning of the century, the Russian revolutionary movement spread also to the Polish territories under Czarist Russia. Its appealing slogans about "proletarian internationalism," about a cosmopolitan, supra-national socialism (the Luxemburgism named after the noted German socialist Rosa Luxemburg who was killed in 1919) even then inflicted great damage on the Polish left. Many socialist leaders, among them Pilsudski, turned to nationalism as a result.

World War I saw Polish opinion radically split. The Germans' occupation of Russian-controlled Polish territory, and their severe treatment of the civilian population,

15

Already in January 1917, President Woodrow Wilson (below) had called for the establishment of "a limited, independent and autonomous Poland," and one of the achievements of the Treaty of Versailles was the reappearance of Poland on the map of Europe, after more than 100 years. On 11 November 1980, a public, if illegal, demonstration took place in Warsaw, to celebrate the 62nd anniversary of liberation (right).

alienated all but the most militaristic pro-Prussian Poles. Following the 1917 Revolution, the Russians' promise to free Poland (but to keep it as a close ally) won the support of workers' and peasants' groups, who called for the restitution of the independent Polish state, but Bolshevism frightened the centrist segments of the population, who placed their hope in the United States and Woodrow Wilson.

Reunification and independence of Polish territory at the end of the war served to bring the social conflicts to the surface. Jozef Pilsudski, the hero who had been imprisoned by the Germans, became head of state and appointed a moderate socialist government that was opposed by groups on both left and right. With the revival of the *Sejm* or parliament, and the holding of legislative elections, democratic processes were restored. But in June 1919 workers' councils were suppressed by the government as part of its anti-Communist campaign. Leftist parties were further weakened and further split

victory of Polish legions under the command of Marshal Pilsudski compelled Russia to cede great chunks of the Ukraine, Belorussia, and Lithuania.

This was not the first time in Poland's history that a more powerful neighbor suffered defeat. Polish kings and feudal lords had often organized marches to the east, and in 1610 even conquered Moscow. In considering the historical background of the present-day anti-Soviet mood in Poland, one must bear in mind that this neighborly antipathy is mutual, and that religious differences also played an important part in it.

The new Polish state which was created after World War I continued to be in an unenviable geopolitical situation. Its extension in the east, the Baltic corridor, the precarious status of the free city of Danzig, the new territories

during the Polish-Soviet war of 1920. Launching their offensive against militarily weak Bolshevik Russia in April, the Poles within only a few days had conquered Kiev and a large part of the Ukraine. But the front was too wide to hold, and under the pressure of Soviet counterattack, they were forced to retreat almost to Warsaw, where in mid-August the decisive battle was fought. The

Newly independent Poland was immediately involved in fighting with Russia on the Eastern frontier. Under Marshal Pilsudski (far left) the population was mobilized to stop the Russian advance. Troops armed with scythes were sent to the front (left). Below, Polish troops being transferred across Germany by rail to the Russian front: on the left the American commission that accompanied them, on the right German military police. Pilsudski's victory over Russia established him as a symbol of Polish liberty: Poles today still cover his tomb with flowers (below, far left).

acquired after the uprising in Silesia, weighed heavily on Poland's relations with her increasingly powerful neighbors, the Soviet Union and Germany.

Internal difficulties also abounded in the Polish republic's early years: agrarian problems, ethnic minorities with their centrifugal tendencies, inflation, strikes, governmental instability. Finally, Pilsudski staged a coup d'état in May 1926 and ruled as dictator, while bearing the title of president, until his death in 1935. He consolidated his position on the right and banned the quickly growing Communist party.

Anti-Sovietism, especially after 1926 when Marshal Pilsudski took power, was the main canon of Poland's foreign policy. It remained unchanged even after Hitler's expansionist intentions became clear.

The Polish government was opposed to the Soviet proposal for the so-called "Eastern pact" in 1934, and in 1935 it declined to join the treaty of alliance with the Soviet Union, France, and Czechoslovakia. Soon thereafter, and largely because of the policy of the then foreign minister Beck, Poland found herself isolated, without any real allies, face to face with the heavily armed German Wehrmacht.

Hitler's attack on Poland, on 1 September 1939, was the beginning of World War II. Poland suffered relatively the highest human losses during the war: more than six million dead, and material destruction estimated at nearly $17 billion ($626 per capita).

In 1939, Stalin got his chance to avenge the defeat of 1920, thanks to his non-aggression pact with Hitler.

After the German invasion, Soviet troops on 17 September 1939 crossed the border into Poland and Polish lands in the east were annexed. A secret agreement had already been signed by Molotov and Ribbentrop, calling for the division of Poland. To ensure that there would be no leftist opposition, and no Communist resistance to this division, Stalin, with the aid of the Comintern, had already dissolved the Polish Communist party (March 1938) and liquidated its leaders—many of whom he ordered shot—together with leading Polish leftists.

The anti-Nazi resistance movement in Poland was therefore organized without any real participation by the Communists. Many of them fled to eastern parts which had been taken, without much resistance, by the Red Army, on 17 September 1939.

The Polish resistance movement against the Germans was in fact organized and led by the middle class, former army officers, the intelligentsia, and the nobility. Many underground organizations continued the tradition of pre-war political parties. After a series of bitter feuds and rivalries, all the rival groups and currents were united into a well-organized Home Army, the *Armia Kraieva* (AK), under the Polish exile government in London.

Millions of Poles who were interned in the Soviet Union asked to join. The U.S.S.R., since Germany's attack on it in June 1941, was now in the war on the Allied side. On the personal intervention of General Wladyslaw Sikorski, the leader of Polish patriots in the west, who arrived in Moscow in December 1941, a Polish division, under the command of General Wladyslaw Anders, was formed in Russia. A year later, General Anders took his units out of the Soviet Union to the Middle East, and subsequently fought, along with the Western Allies, on the European front.

In 1943 a particularly gruesome case of Russian oppression came to light, the so-called Katyn massacre. The Soviets, on agreeing to the formation of General Anders' Polish army in 1941, released 448 Polish officers who had

The German onslaught on Poland was short and intense—the first "Blitzkrieg." Warsaw surrendered on 27 September, and fighting had ceased by early October. Poland was then effectively partitioned again, between Germany and Russia, according to an agreement reached in Moscow on 28 September. A rare photograph (left) shows Hitler's entry into Warsaw, while below, German troops are seen breaking down a frontier barrier on 1 September.

been held in camps in Russia since the Soviet invasion of Poland in September 1939. Anders knew, however, that 9,361 officers were listed as being imprisoned in Russia. The nearly 9,000 missing officers, according to Stalin, had escaped to Manchuria. Then, in April 1943, in the Katyn Forest, the Germans on their Russian offensive announced that they had discovered the mass graves of Polish officers, inmates of one of the Soviet-held camps, who had been killed in 1940. When the Polish government in exile in London asked the Red Cross to investigate, the Soviets broke diplomatic relations with them. Upon General Sikorski's death in an airplane crash in Gibraltar, Stanislaw Mikolajczyk, leader of the Peasant party, became head of the Polish government in London. General Sikorski had favored normalization of relations with Russia. Stalin, however, was in no hurry to resurrect the Polish Communist party. In Poland, therefore, the

To this very day, the circumstances under which many Communist leaders lost their lives have still not been brought to light. According to the official version, the founder and first secretary of the Polish Workers' party, Nowotko, was murdered by another leading Communist, a hero from the Spanish civil war, Boleslaw Molojec. But other sources say that both Molojec and his younger brother were victims of a conspiracy organized by Moscow.

Nor did Nowotko's successor, Pawel Finder, fare any better. Together with several other members of the Polish Workers' party, he fell into the hands of the Gestapo and was shot. Only the third successive secretary, Wladyslaw Gomulka, survived the war and managed to stay at the head of the party from 1943 to 1948.

Poland suffered throughout the war, enduring the long-

left went ahead and started to organize small resistance units which were later united into the National Guard. Thus the People's Army, *Armia Ludewa* (AL), came into being.

An attempt to form the Polish Workers' party (to succeed the Communist party which Stalin dissolved) was made in January 1942. It was dictated by the necessity to control various leftist groups, but mainly to set up receiving centers for the Soviet agents working inside Germany.

But continually, from the start, the organizers and the leaders of the new Polish Communist party became engaged in factional strife. Moscow encouraged disunity by continuing to oppose the creation of a broader popular front, and by preventing cooperation with the rival Home Army, the AK.

22

The defeat of Poland did not mean the end of resistance. General Sikorski (left) became commander in chief of the Polish forces outside Poland, as well as prime minister of the government in exile, till his death in an airplane crash in 1943. Polish troops fought in western Europe, notably at Monte Cassino, and also on the Eastern Front. Resistance within Poland was continuous, culminating in the Warsaw Rising of 1944 (below).

est, hardest German occupation. The country was covered with extermination camps—in Auschwitz alone, about four million people were put to death, mostly Jews from all over Europe. Terror and genocide hardened resistance and strengthened the movement. But they failed to forge national unity. As the war was drawing to an end, the conflicts between the two principal groups—pro-Western and pro-Soviet—became fiercer.

Confronted with the fact that the offensive by the Soviet army brought along the danger of Communist rule, the government in London was preparing the national uprising whose ultimate goal was to prevent the Bolshevization of Poland. Without any support from the Allies, the chief command of the Home Army (AK) started the Warsaw uprising on 1 August 1944, just as the Red Army was approaching the capital. Thanks to long preparations, good organization, and great courage, the

insurgents succeeded in freeing a large part of the city and strengthening their defense. An airlift was set up. But it was in fact a suicidal act. And it ended in one of the greatest tragedies in Polish history.

Only the Vistula River separated the insurgents from the Red Army which had arrived at the Praga district on the right bank in September—the same district that witnessed the blood bath at Russian hands in 1794. Soldiers of the First Polish Army (formed in the Soviet Union) helplessly watched the thick clouds of black smoke over Warsaw which was burning out in an unequal battle. The one and only attempt to force the river was paid dearly: 3,764 men, mainly soldiers from the Polish units with the Red Army, were either killed or wounded.

After two months of heroic resistance, the commander of the uprising, Bar Komarowski, signed the capitulation. The insurgents were taken war prisoners; the population was interned and sent to concentration camps; and War-

saw, on personal order from Adolf Hitler, was leveled to the ground. More than 200,000 were killed, among them 18,000 insurgents.

The Polish government in exile in London not only lost the military battle; it lost the political struggle as well. Under the patronage of the Red Army, the Communists were taking over. Anti-Communist resistance groups

were ruthlessly liquidated. On 11 February 1945, in accordance with the Yalta agreement, a coalition "Provisional Government of National Unity" was formed. Stanislaw Mikolajczyk was brought in as representative of the London government. But two years later, Poland's future was sealed when the "Democratic Bloc" consisting of the Polish Workers' party, the Polish Socialist party, the Peasant party, and the Democratic party won the election for a new parliament or *Sejm*. Once more, Mikolajczyk was forced into exile, and in Poland, the persecutions of opposition parties and of former Home Army resistance fighters began.

World War II radically changed the geopolitical picture of Central Europe. At Potsdam, the Allies gave de facto

The shape of postwar Poland was largely determined at the conferences of Yalta (February 1945) and Potsdam (August 1945). At Yalta, Stalin, Roosevelt, and Churchill (below) established Poland's eastern frontier (below right: the map used at the conference), and at Potsdam the western frontier was settled. But for Poland itself the immediate priority was reconstruction after five years of occupation and subjection, and the destruction caused during the liberation. Right: the Castle Square in Warsaw, with Sigismund's

Column already reconstructed. Political activity also resumed. Stanislaw Mikolajczyk, then vice premier and leader of the Polish Peasant Party is seen (bottom, far left of picture) checking his registration to vote in a referendum on 30 June 1946, the first time Poles had voted since 1938. The issues involved the abolition of the senate, approval of land reforms and industrial nationalization, and consolidation of the western frontier.

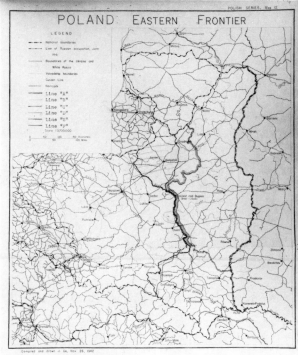

recognition to Poland's new frontier with Germany (Oder/Neisse). The frontier with the Soviet Union, with slight changes, went along the Curzon line. The change of frontiers resulted in the eviction of Germans from East Prussia, Pomerania, and Silesia and the mass exodus of Poles from the territories ceded to the Soviet Union. More than twenty million people were affected by it. It was the largest migration in the history of our era.

Fratricidal battles, Soviet control of all sectors of life, oppression and persecutions of former resistance fighters, of the aristocracy, and of the peasantry, paved the way for ruthless Stalinist rule. By 1948, Communist power was firmly established. But differences and disagreements within the leadership of the party became more distinct. Gomulka was opposed to the unification of the Polish Workers' party and the Polish Socialist party. He was also against the setting up of the Cominform (Communist

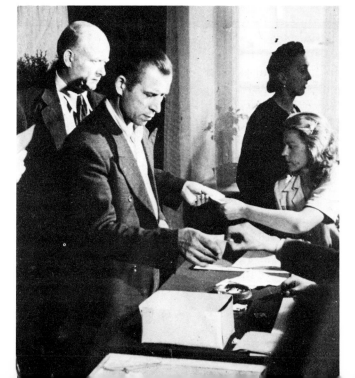

Information Bureau, formed in October 1947 to "coordinate" activities of European Communist parties), which he rightly saw as a new center for Soviet control of the Communist movement, designed to curtail the independence of young socialist states in Eastern Europe. Other Communist countries faced similar dilemmas. Only the Yugoslavians, under Tito, rebelled openly and went their own way. In Poland, however, the pro-Soviet faction won.

Gomulka and many leading Communist figures were purged. In December 1948, the Communist and the Socialist party merged into the Polish United Worker's Party, and Boleslaw Bierut, the man who was more pliable and more suitable to Moscow, was put at its head. Today, in the jargon of Polish Communists, the period from 1948 to 1956 is still known as the "time of errors and distortions." Though less brutal than in other East European countries, Stalinism in Poland left deep traces. The first five-year plan, from 1950 to 1955, was a faithful copy of the Soviet pattern. Break-neck industrialization was accompanied by collectivization. Huge investment was too heavy a burden for a country totally devastated by the war. Thus Poland was forced to import economic and political solutions totally alien to her historical experience and national tradition. Political and personal freedom was stifled. Arbitrary rule by state bureaucracy, and terror under the secret police, completed the picture of an intolerable, totalitarian regime.

But Moscow obviously felt that it was not enough to exert indirect influence (through the Communist party) and control (through its advisers). To be absolutely sure, Stalin sent Konstantin Rokosowski, the Soviet Marshal, to take charge of Poland's ministry of defense. His Polish origin was used as a pretext. But Poland was the only

The general election of 19 January 1947 (below: a display of posters just before the elections) was violently contested, with reports of 24 deaths in about 50 terrorist attacks during the campaign. The headquarters of the Communist party in Warsaw (right) was protected by guards armed with submachine guns during the campaign.

Communist country which had a Soviet Marshal as minister of defense.

The death of Stalin in 1953 and Khrushchev's dramatic revelations at the Twentieth Party Congress three years after set off a more relaxed political trend throughout Eastern Europe. In Poland, however, it soon confronted the regime with the first workers' demonstrations, street violence, and an eruption of popular feeling. In June 1956 the local authorities in Poznan refused to negotiate with the workers from the Cegielski factory.

It started as a peaceful demonstration in Poznan, on what was then Stalin Square, in June 1956. Thousands of people were awaiting news from the delegation of workers who had gone to Warsaw to talk to the government in an attempt to settle the labor dispute.

Once again, the authorities tried to frighten and humiliate the demonstrators. But the crowd, provoked by the arrogance of power, turned and stormed the nearby prison, released the prisoners, seized arms, and fought their way to the headquarters of the secret police. The official figure for the dead and wounded of that battle was not released until August 1981—when the names of over seventy victims were engraved on the monument built in memory of them by the present workers of Poznan.

The Poznan riots were brutally suppressed by tanks. But the tragedy brought the mounting political crisis to a head—the Party was shaken and the leadership split. Pressure for reforms continued to mount.

The Democratic Bloc, consisting of the Communist party and its allies, made every effort to ensure victory. Demonstrations, like the one below, became a daily occurence in Warsaw. The result was a vote of 80 percent for the Democratic Bloc. On 5 February Boleslaw Bierut (left), leader of the Communist party, took the oath as President of the Republic.

In July, the Central Committee met. Headed by a moderate, Edward Ochab, who became first secretary of the Party on Bierut's death, it still tried to put the blame on "anti-socialist forces" for the tragic events. However, it did admit that there were justifiable grounds for popular dissatisfaction.

Poland was in dire need of a new leader—someone the people could trust. Wladyslaw Gomulka seemed the obvious man: he had been the victim of Stalinism, and bore an aura of martyrdom—a sure point in his favor. He was also a Communist of long standing, which offered sufficient guarantee that he would not tolerate excessive deviations from the Party line. He was accordingly rehabilitated and reinstated into the Party, from which he had been formally expelled in 1948.

But the situation in the country continued to deteriorate; the leadership, under mounting popular pressure, torn by internal friction, was rapidly losing control. The threat of Soviet military intervention hung heavy on the air as the Central Committee assembled for the eighth plenary session on 19 October 1956, and, on Ochab's proposal, welcomed back the victims of the earlier Stalinist purges: Gomulka, Spychalski, Kliszko, and Loga-Sowinski.

On that same morning, without prior notice, the Soviet leadership—Khrushchev, Kaganovic, Molotov, and Mikoyan—descended on Warsaw. The Central Committee plenum was interrupted, and the Polish Politburo (the executive committee of the Party), including Gomulka, went out to meet their uninvited visitors. They spent the entire day and night arguing, enduring

As Poland's geographical location, between Germany and Russia, has had so great an effect on her political history, so has her spiritual location, between German Protestantism and Russian Orthodoxy affected her religious history. The deep identification of the Polish people with their religion (right: during the Millenary celebrations in 1964, a mass before the Black Madonna of Czestochowa) reached a peak in June 1979, when a Polish Pope returned to his country. Below: a welcoming crucifix held aloft in the Castle Square, Warsaw.

insults from an enraged Khrushchev, and trying to convince the Russians that they were capable of resolving the crisis without their "fraternal aid." The Russians were particularly angry that the Poles had neither consulted nor informed them of the leadership changes. Later, in discussing the meeting, Politburo member Zawadski told

the Central Committee: "From the start, we took the view that this was an internal matter for our Party and its Central Committee. We did everything to calm down our Soviet comrades. We tried to explain the essence, the sense of democratization, now in course, and the impossibility for it to be reversed."
The Polish Central Committee listened in total silence.

Finally, Artur Strewicz put a direct question to Marshal Rokosowski: "What was the object of Soviet troop movements in the direction of Warsaw, on the western frontier and in the region of Wroclaw? Was the Polish leadership informed of it?" he asked. Rokosowski, still at that time Poland's minister of defense, admitted that there had been "some movement" of Soviet troops, and that he had demanded that Marshal Koniew stop the northern group and order them to return to their garrison. But by then it was clear that the Soviet leaders had already decided against the use of military force. The uprising in Hungary, that same Autumn, had been ruthlessly crushed by Soviet tanks. In Poland, however, the Soviets were made to realize how much it would cost.
The Polish leaders won their case. Gomulka's return to the helm of the Party held out the promise of change: "Workers of Poznan did not rebel against People's Poland, or against socialism," he told the Central Committee on election, "they protested against the evil which got into our social system and which offended them deeply.... It would be politically naive to try to present this tragedy as the work of imperialist forces and of provocateurs. The causes of the Poznan tragedy, of the profound dissatisfaction of our working class, lie in us, in the leadership of the Party, in the government."
Gomulka's comeback was received with great enthusiasm: the "Polish October" was seen as a historic turning point in the socialist evolution of Poland. There was euphoria among university students, artists, and the intelligentsia. It was as if the whole country had suddenly come to life. Traditional satirical cabaret was revived, and the door opened widely and wildly to Western fashions. The parliamentary elections of January 1957 offered an increased list of candidates and secured greater participation of non-Party members; there were Catholics and representatives from other national parties set up to protect sectional interests. In the new *Sejm*, besides 239 deputies of the Polish United Workers' Party (Communists), there were 118 from the United Peasant Alliance, 39 Democratic Alliance, and 63 independents.

In the immediate postwar years, people spoke with great passion about the rebirth of Poland, which had regained its ancient historic frontiers. The northern and western lands which, until the end of World War II, had belonged to the Third Reich, were actually the territories of the old Polish Piast dynasty.

The Ukrainians, Byelorussians, and Lithuanians—nations which represented compact and often troublesome ethnic minorities in Poland between the two World wars—remained inside the Soviet Union. Thus, after many centuries, the question of to whom Poland belonged—which had been the source of numerous historical conflicts—was settled. The Poles could at last say that it was their own state, in continuation of their thousand-year-old tradition. However rhetorical this may sound, this solution has been a constant inspiration to national awareness and self-confidence, even despite the fact that Poland's sovereignty continues to be limited by the U.S.S.R.

The deep patriotism of these early years filled and inspired

all aspects of public life—especially in the cultural and scientific fields. The Millennium of the Polish State was celebrated with great pomp, and old spiritual and artistic values were rediscovered and resurrected. "Socialist realism" never took root in Polish art. The dilemmas and tragedies of young Poles, who, in the war-time resistance, had to choose between two rival groups—the People's Army and the Home Army—became obsessive subjects in the literary and artistic creations of the late forties and fifties.

The appearance of *Po Prostu* magazine, whose editors introduced themselves as a "group of discontented people, calling for better and more," was a protest reaction against Stalinism. "The system of distortions is widely spread," they wrote. "It has crept into cities, villages, farms, factories, and offices—even into people's minds." This dedicated group of intellectuals set out to "destroy such a system" so that the people would again become aware of their power.

The Polish October ushered in a cultural renaissance.

Andrzejewski wrote his famous novel *Darkness Hides the
Earth* about the Spanish Inquisition destroying people
most devoted to Christian ideas. It was then that K. Bran-
dys wrote the *Defense of Granada* and the *Mother of Kings*:
that Roman Brandstaetter wrote his play *The Silence,* and
J. Broszkiewicz, *The Names of Power*: that Roman Bratny
wrote *Komumbowi.*

The Second Exhibition of Contemporary Art was an
exciting display of avant-garde painting hitherto unprecedented in the Soviet Bloc. A whole generation of
modern painters, Fangora, Gierowski, Tarasin, Kantor,
and others, came to stay. The festival of contemporary
music, "Warsaw Autumn," introduced new artists—
Baird, Penderecki, Kotowski, and Lutowlawski.

While the trend of free creation and experiment continued, more or less successfully, in culture and arts, the
sixties brought new failures and disappointments in political, social, and economic life. At first, Gomulka gave his
support to many of the ideas of the Polish October, but
later, however, it seems that either he did not fully understand them, that he was deliberately holding back and
slowing down, fearing that such liberalization would
become uncontrollable internally, or cause new complica-
tions in relations with Moscow. The ideas of Professor
Lange and of other reformist-minded economists were
met with dogged resistance by the bureaucrats. And
Gomulka grew increasingly mistrustful of his former colleagues and followers.

*The official attitude to the Church has varied over the years, but was never worse than following the war, when the new Constitution nationalized Church property, and many of the clergy were imprisoned. But the demolishing of the official Church totally failed to destroy Catholicism in the country; it merely went "underground," and private houses have been illegally converted to places of worship, such as this one in Opole Stare (*Left; interior *below) in the east of Poland.*

Once again, autocratic methods of government were stifling every initiative. The expectations of the vast majority of Polish intelligentsia were frustrated. Enthusiasm fade, alienation followed, and, in the end, the intelligentsia and Gomulka's regime stood on two opposite sides. Poland is the home of a long tradition in self-government. It is no accident, therefore, that in all crucial junctures, or at critical moments, the idea has been revived and pushed to the fore as an alternative to the centralized system of government. Thus, in the restless fifties, the workers took the initiative, in a spontaneous movement, for self-management. Fearful that such uncontrolled formation of factory councils could lead to the disintegration of the whole system, in November 1956, without any thorough preparations, the new leadership set up a framework for official workers' councils. But the new law only limited their scope and rights. Right from the start, elections for the councils were reduced to a farcical formality. Instead of democratically elected bodies, what emerged was an oligarchy of four—the managing director, the trade union chairman, the workers' council chairman, and, of course, the Party secretary. And, just as in

1948 and 1949, it was the trade unions themselves that played the principal role in the final liquidation of self-management.

Thus, little by little, the gains of the Polish October withered away. At the end of 1967, under the guise of the "struggle against Zionism," an ugly wave of purges swept across the country. Polish Jews—many of them prominent academics, scientists, economists, even high-ranking government officials—were forced out of their jobs, and subsequently out of the country. The purge was part and parcel of a wider campaign against "contemporary revisionism," in effect, against the intelligentsia, now openly and increasingly critical of Gomulka's policy, its economic failures, and the resulting deteriorating standard of living. Poland was moving toward a new crisis, but Gomulka refused to budge.

In May 1968, the students of Warsaw University staged a demonstration following the banning of a play by Adam Mickiewicz, *Dziadi.* Police and security forces moved to the university compound, and after several days of fighting, the demonstrations were suppressed. Some of Poland's most brilliant scholars—among them

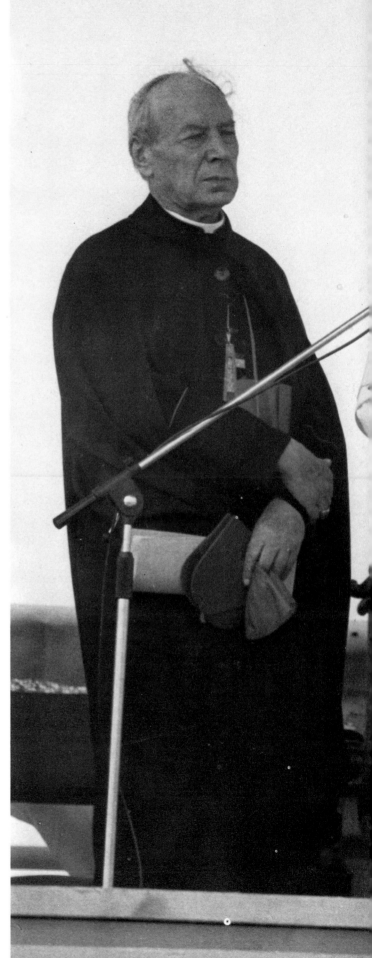

16 October 1978 and a new Pope is named. But the conclave had confounded all expectations with their choice; the former Cardinal Wojtyla, metropolitan of Cracow, the first non-Italian Pope for 455 years and, moreover, from Communist Poland. In Cracow itself, in the midst of the general jubilation, his portrait hangs in the window of his residence the day after the stunning announcement.

Kolakowski, Schaff, and Bauman—left the country in protest. The leaders of the students' unrest suffered reprisals. Among these were Adam Michnik, Jacek Kuron, and Karol Modzelewski—the later founders of KOR (Workers' Self-Defense Committee)—who in 1980 were to exert a strong influence on the Solidarity movement. The Soviet intervention in Czechoslovakia that same year only deepened the nationwide somber apathy. The social and economic crisis which had been slowly building up for years was gathering speed. Pep speeches and appeals for unity could hardly have bridged the widening gap. Attempts in 1969 and 1970 to correct some of the glaring defects of economic planning made no difference. The new five-year modernization program (1971–1975) contained many elements of economic reform—calling for more sacrifice and more work—but without any immediate prospect of living standards going up. Inevitably, it provoked suspicion and resistance from the start. By Christmas, when steep food price increases were announced, it had triggered off a new explosion.

On 14 December 1970 riots broke out in Gdansk. In the

Pope John Paul, on his visit to Poland in June 1979, gathered vast crowds around him—at the mass he conducted in honor of St. Stanislaw (Poland's patron saint) there were an estimated two million people. Left: side by side with his former superior, Primate Cardinal Wyszynski, the man responsible for the Vatican's recognition of Polish frontiers, and (below) students of the Catholic University of Lublin in a particularly enthusiastic moment.

Lenin shipyard, workers struck in protest over the new price increases and marched to the Voyvodship Party committee demanding to speak to the Party secretary. Provoked by official response, in a raging outburst of anger, they burnt down the Party headquarters and a railway station, and demolished shops and public buildings. In Warsaw, the leadership panicked. Special army and security forces were rushed to the Baltic, but there seems to have been no coordination between political and military decision makers. Stanislaw Kocilek was sent by the Politburo with instructions to persuade the strikers to return to work. They trusted him and responded to his appeal. What he did not know, however, was that in the meantime, the army was ordered to cordon off all approaches to factories and shipyards.

On 15 December, in response to his appeal, the workers arrived by early morning train. On their way to the shipyard, they were stopped by security forces who had orders to shoot; many workers were killed. The Party commission which conducted the official investigation that followed submitted its report a long time ago. But,

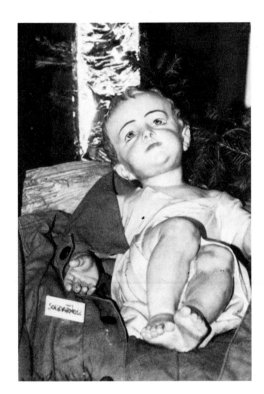

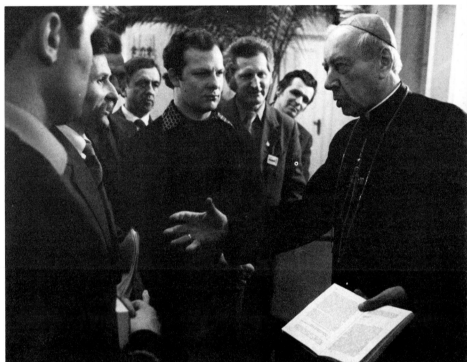

despite public pressure, the true causes and responsibilities for the tragedy have still not been brought to light.

Fourteen years earlier, Wladyslaw Gomulka sided with the workers against the abuse of Communist power, thereby winning national confidence and support. Now, he personified the power which, with equal brutality, had crushed the revolt in Gdansk. Though there could be no doubt of his personal responsibility for the tragic consequences, he was allowed to step down under the pretext of ill health. With Gomulka went also his closest associates in the Politburo—Kliszko, Jaszczuk, Marshal Spychalski, and subsequently, Premier Josef Cyrankiewicz and the chairman of trade unions, Ignacy Loga-Sowinski, too. Thus closed another era which started with high hopes and ended with revolt.

Edward Gierek, a man who in the later years of Gomul-

ka's rule had played an increasingly important role, took his place. His power base was Katowice. His stronghold was the miners: he himself had started his career as a miner in France and Belgium, and so he understood their mentality and defended their interests. He also had the reputation of a politician who gets things done.

In 1931 he had joined the French Communist party. He took part in the French and Belgian resistance, and spent many years in Western Europe. All this was later to help him to establish good personal relationships with Western politicians and businessmen, and to restore Poland's traditional links with the West, especially France. His athletic presence, his talent for plain speaking, his instinct for the crowds, and his flair for the theatrical won him wide popularity. He presented to the nation the spectacularly daring and ambitious policy of "dynamic growth," promising to improve living standards quickly and radi-

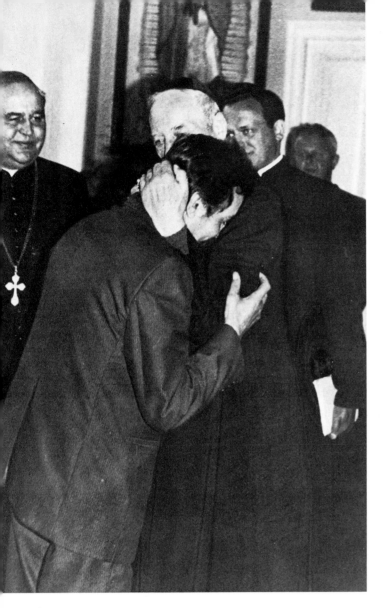

cally. In the Poland of 1971, this is what the people wanted above all.

Gomulka's era had been stamped by relatively slow economic growth and austerity. Himself scrupulously honest, with a reputation for thriftiness and modesty, he not only demanded the same from his aids and from his administration, but from the nation too. For ten years, from 1960 to 1970, real wages were increasing at a rate of a mere 1.8 percent annually. It was one of the lowest growth rates in Europe.

In constrast, Gierek's administration saw the prospect of fast economic development. It used the considerable reserves left by Gierek's predecessor, and foreign credits, now easily obtainable; it enjoyed the advantages of a good harvest and of world market prices for Polish exports. The national income rate continued to grow, and in the first two years, real wages went up by 12 percent. Industry was modernized: new technology imported from the West doubled the production capacity. It was a success, which, when it collapsed ten years later, people said had gone to Gierek's head.

The high rate of growth was kept up. Although internal reserves had been exhausted, and the looming energy crisis was obvious, the Polish government pressed on unheedingly with its strategy of "dynamic growth." Maintaining and even accelerating the rate of investment meant borrowing more. In 1973, Poland owed the West only $2.5 billion. By 1976, the Polish debt rose to $11

Scenes showing the Russians giving "fraternal aid" to their fellow Communists in Hungary. In 1956, following the government's announcement of withdrawal from the Warsaw Pact, Budapest was briefly controlled by the Hungarians (right) but the Russians soon returned in force (below). All in all, more than 160,000 Hungarian refugees fled across the country's borders.

billion, to reach, four years later, over $20 billion. This was used not only for the purchase of machines and consumer goods, but also for raw material imports. The enormous investment boom exceeded national raw material capacity. Then a succession of disastrous harvests, together with bad farm policy, made food imports a stark necessity, and this, in turn, necessitated more borrowing, with the result that Poland's debt soon exceeded $23 billion.

Agriculture had been neglected—only 4 percent of industrial production was intended for it, which meant that food production continued to stagnate because of shortages of machines and fertilizers. In 1970, Poland imported 2.7 million tons of grain: in 1978, food imports rose to over 8 million tons. At the same time, government policy, which favored state farms, deepened the gulf between the regime and private farmers.

Seventy-five percent of the arable land in Poland is in pri-

vate hands, supplying more than 80 percent of the country's food. But, throughout those years, the private farmers could count on only one-fifth of the total agricultural investment. While 40,000 machines were idling or rotting on state farms—either due to shortage of spare parts or simple human neglect and carelessness—private farmers could not buy even the simplest, old-fashioned farm tools. What is more, the price they were paid for delivering food to the state was below production cost: but they were forced to sell as this entitled them to purchase fertilizers, seed, coal, and cement—essentials no farmer can go without. This was really compulsory purchase in disguise.

As a consequence of this policy, 1.5 million people left farming during Gierek's rule. Since the early 1970s, infla-

tion had become increasingly apparent. In spite of it, price policy remained practically unchanged. Shortages of food, especially of meat, the price of which was frozen in 1970, became chronic. On the other hand, prices for some industrial goods and of public services went up, even as much as 100 to 150 percent.

An attempt to stop this trend was made in June 1976. But it was done without advance consultation, and without any serious thorough preparation: it was doomed as soon as the new prices were introduced. Compensations offered to the lowest income groups were inadequate. The so-called "democratic consultations" had been merely a fiction designed to buffer the effect. Factory meetings convened to approve the price increases turned into strikes and protest demonstrations: the most violent in the Ursus tractor plant, where the workers overturned a locomotive and blocked the international railway line. In Radom, there were street riots, and the party headquarters was set on fire.

That same evening Premier Piotr Jaroszewicz revoked the decision, admitting before television cameras that his government had made a mistake by going ahead with

price increases. But even though so obviously shaken by public reaction, the government nevertheless went on behaving as if it did not have a crisis on its hands. Official propaganda was soon blasting away, blaming trouble-makers and enemies of the state, while the situation continued to deteriorate. Repisals against the leaders of the strikes at Ursus and Radom provoked a wave of protests among intellectuals. The dissidents, until that time better known outside than inside Poland, set up a committee for the defense of workers (KOR), which was to play an important role in subsequent events. Its founders, Jacek Kuron and Adam Michnik, had been active in the students' movement of the sixties, and played a leading role in Warsaw University demonstrations in 1968. Others, like the well-known writer Jerzy Andrejewski and economist Edward Lipinski, provided the distinction of national figures of an older generation.

At the same time, unofficial groups, the flying universities, underground publications and publishing houses, theaters, and political cabarets were making themselves felt on the intellectual scene and beyond.

On the initiative of KOR and other dissidents the first cells of the free union movement were being set up in many factories. In the villages, too, the peasants were beginning to organize their own union to defend their rights. The Roman Catholic church played a particularly important role in those years. Cardinal Stefan Wyszynski's great personal authority always provided inspiration and guidance—in moments of crisis, his was the decisive voice. When passions had to be restrained, when Poland's national survival was at stake, the nation listened to him. The Church has left a strong stamp on Polish history. Its influence, always strong, was especially so whenever Polish national interests were threatened—as they had been previously by Protestant Germany and Orthodox Russia. And so Catholicism became identified with patriotism, deeply rooted in the Polish mentality, and it remains in the national character today.

During World War II, the Church shared the fate of the nation and the trials of occupation. The priests joined the resistance movement and several thousand of them perished in German concentration camps. Then when the war ended, the Soviet-installed Communist regime set out to break what it saw as a formidable opponent of its doctrine; but even during the harshest years, the Communists could not silence its voice.

Poznan in the aftermath of the riots there in June 1956 (left): *three divisions of tanks had been called in, and the exact number of dead and wounded civilians is still not known. This photograph was taken at some risk: the figure at far right, back to the camera, is a member of the patrol of secret police.*

After Poznan, the regime was obliged to make drastic policy changes, manifested by the reinstatement and promotion of Wladyslaw Gomulka (right) *to leader of the Party. He immediately won wide popularity with his new liberal policies, and a wave of enthusiasm for news of further developments quickly spread among workers and students* (below).

The new Constitution deprived the Church of many of its former privileges, nationalizing its estates, separating Church from state, and otherwise restricting its activity. But in fact this only served to strengthen the Church's standing. When Cardinal Wyszynski was imprisoned, it strengthened his authority.

Gomulka recognized this. The first thing he did on returning to power was to order Wyszynski's release. In return, Wyszynski lent his immense authority in support of Gomulka's policy. The only thing the two men had in common was that they were both Polish patriots and, in their different ways, working for the same goal—Poland's independence.

The change, when it came, was fast and spectacular. Within a month an agreement was signed formalizing a new relationship between the Communist government and the Roman Catholic hierarchy. Religion was again taught in state-run schools. Cardinal Wyszynski received a passport to visit Rome – normalization between Socialist Poland and the Vatican was in the offing.

But this period of cooperation and compromise did not last long. By the end of 1957, it was already breaking up. The government's refusal to broadcast the Primate's traditional Christmas message on the national radio network provoked a sharp protest by the Church. Cardinal Wyszynski was personally offended, and this led him to call on the Catholics to boycott municipal elections. This was the first test of strength. Gomulka retaliated by accusing the Church of using religion for political ends and of attempting to turn the believers against socialism. One thing led to another. In July, police raided the Jasna Gora monastery, the holy national shrine of the Black

The new hope that Gomulka had once instilled in Poland slowly turned to disillusion and bitterness. Eventually feelings reached breaking point, and after an announcement of increases of 10–30 percent in the price of food at Christmas, 1970, the Gdansk shipyard workers went on strike (above), soon to be followed by others from Gdynia and Szczecin. Then the strike turned to riots in Gdansk, and soon got out of control; shops were looted and set on fire.

The government's reply took the form of specially trained security forces (on parade, right) who were rushed to the scene. They need never have been sent, because on 15 December the workers voted to return peacefully to work following a government appeal. But on their way there that morning, the troops opened fire on them.

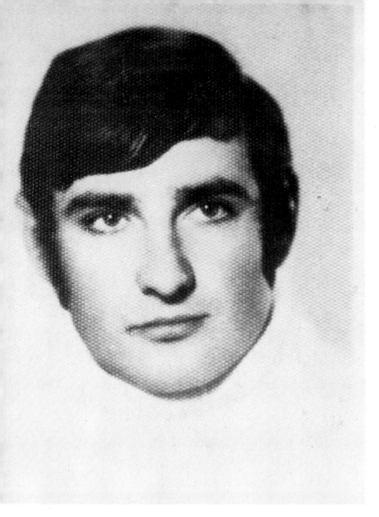

Even the ultra-conservative official figures list forty-five deaths as a result of the massacre in Gdansk. Weeping wives and girlfriends are pictured below, but it was not until ten years later that men such as Pawloski (left) were to be formally remembered on a monument in their honor.

Smoke in Gdansk: 19 buildings (including the Party headquarters) and 220 shops were set on fire by thre rioters, according to government statistics; behavior which the Solidarity movement of 1980 was careful to avoid repeating. In the Eastern Bloc, violent riots all meet with the same result—armed police and tanks (above).

45

Gomulka's successor, Gierek (opposite page, left) *set about a whirlwind change in the Polish economy injected with vast loans of foreign money. Huge invest-ments were made in the fields of industry and urbani-zation, whereas agriculture, except on the still totally inefficient state farms, was neglected. These apartment blocks in Warsaw* (right) *reflect the short-sightedness and haphazardness of his whole policy: ten years after their construction, they are crumbling away.*

Madonna, and accused the Polish episcopate of publish-ing anti-state literature. At the Party congress in March 1959, Gomulka launched a fierce attack on the Church, demanding it withdraw within strictly defined religious boundaries. The conflict sharpened. It intensified even after Wyszynski and Gomulka met in the spring of 1960, and began to look more and more like a clash between two powerful personalities rather than between two incompatible ideologies.

The climax came in January 1961. The Central Com-mittee decided that religion would no longer be taught in schools, and from there on both sides dug their heels. Gomulka's fall offered a new chance for a *modus vivendi* between Church and Communist authority. The country was in turmoil: the regime was shaken, and Gierek needed the support of the Church. The cardinal granted it. In his Christmas Homily, the Polish Primate called for "restraint and patient work for the renewal." This, he said, was not the time for anger and revenge. "We must forgive because each of us is responsible for past mis-takes." He warned against the witch-hunt that might provoke new tensions and great dangers. In parliament, the new premier, Piotr Jaroszewicz, pledged to work for a realistic understanding with the Church. The episcopate responded with a New Year message which contained its conditions: return of property which was nationalized or confiscated; construction of new churches and recon-struction of old ones; an independent Catholic press; and resumption of Catholic clubs and associations.

Relations with the Vatican were improving. Monsignor Casaroli was a frequent visitor to Poland, and talks on the former German dioceses of Olstyn, Gorzow, Wroclaw, and Opole were brought to a successful conclusion. In June 1972, the Vatican handed them over to Polish bishops, thus formally recognizing the Polish frontier on the Oder and the Neisse which Cardinal Wyszynski had fought for. "The frontiers of the new bishoprics are iden-tical with state frontiers; thus, the tireless efforts of Polish bishops have been crowned," he told Jaroszewicz.

Poland is today divided into 27 bishoprics and has 20,000 priests. There are 18,000 church centers for religious edu-cation, with 80 percent of schoolchildren receiving religi-ous education.

In December 1977, when Edward Gierek visited the Vatican, he was able to tell Pope Paul VI that the authorities and the clergy had come to terms because for both Church and state "great national aims" were upper-most. The other man who, besides Cardinal Wyszynski, played a significant role in bringing all this about, was the second man of the Polish church, the metropolitan of Cracow, Cardinal Karol Wojtyla, who in October 1978 became Pope John Paul II.

His visit to Poland in June 1979 may have precipitated that slight climatic change that is sometimes sufficient to change the landscape of a country. One thing is certain— the Catholic church's position has become much stronger as a result. Despite the disastrous failures of Gierek's policies, it is to his credit that he recognized the Church,

Public feeling about the tragic events in Poland in the last four decades continues to ride high today. This banner in the Powazki cemetery on All Souls Day, 1980, commemorates the living memories of 1944, 1956, 1970, and 1976, and celebrates the rising tide of workers' rights under Solidarity.

and, throughout the ten years of his rule, kept a business-like relationship with it. Were it not for that, the events which brought down his regime might have taken a more tragic course.

But Gierek had wasted his great chance of December 1970. And in doing so, he provided indisputable arguments in favor of the democratic forces which today lead the national movement for Poland's renewal.

K. S. KAROL

The Peaceful Revolution

Workers in a moment of relaxation during the strike at the Lenin shipyard (right), *which rapidly became the focus of the labor unrest in August 1980. As the scene of unprecendented negotiations between a Communist government and striking workers, it acquired an almost symbolic importance. Crowds flocked to its flower-covered gates to talk to the striking workers* (below), *or just to wait on events* (overleaf, pp. 50–51).

a bit of personal evidence. In July 1979, I was among journalists accompanying the French foreign minister, Jean-François Poncet, to Warsaw. Thanks to some Polish friends I was able to read the shorthand minutes of a meeting at Jablonna attended by the principal economists of the Party and its subsections, who were contemplating the future with fear and bewilderment. The country's economy even then was comparable to an overcrowded train rushing down the wrong track. It was heading straight for total disaster, and meanwhile, even before the catastrophe occurred, the Poles' everyday life, was becoming daily more wretched and demoralizing. During the previous winter, a spell of cold weather—though less extreme than the official announcement led to believe—

Since 1953, Eastern Europe has witnessed a whole series of popular outbursts; but none of them had ever given rise to an organized and independent workers' movement. Then, last year in Poland, a totally peaceful protest action, without a single loss of life, resulted in the birth of "Solidarity," the first worker-run union in the history of the Soviet bloc. It is an event sure to figure in history books as one of the most important of the century, one which marks, to my mind, the first real break with the theory and the institutions of Stalinism, which still rule the U.S.S.R. and the other socialist republics. It is no exaggeration, then, to say that since last summer, Poland has been experiencing a peaceful revolution with international consequences. But before examining its implications, it is necessary to understand how the Polish workers succeeded in organizing themselves despite their totalitarian system, and how they imposed changes which only yesterday would have been unthinkable.

By way of answering this question I would like to relate

was enough to paralyze all production. Lack of fuel—
even though Poland is a great exporter of coal—brought
industry and transport to a standstill for a whole week.
The resulting losses equaled those of an earthquake. No
one in Warsaw failed to realize that discontent was growing among the workers. But of course no one, not even
the dissident intellectuals, could have expected anything
other than a strike movement like those of the past, conducted entirely within the system: the workers might
leave the factories, might even destroy a local Party headquarters, but in the end they would entrust that same
Party with the task of improving matters.

Contrary to all expectations, the strike movement that
broke out at the beginning of July 1980 took an unprecedented form. It all began with the unobtrusive and
ambiguous announcement of an increase in the price of
meat intended for distribution in the factories. In the
suburbs of Warsaw, at the Ursus tractor factory renowned
for its violent strikes in 1976, work stopped immediately

in several workrooms. The next day, the same thing happened at Zeran, a large car assembly plant which had
played a prominent part in the disturbances of 1956. But
the government proved more accommodating than it had
been in the past: representatives arrived on the scene,
agreed to raise wages, and even postponed an announced
increase in the price of bacon. Although all communica-
tion between factories is forbidden in Poland, the news
nevertheless spread by word of mouth, and also by means
of KOR (Workers' Self-Defense Committee), the role of
which will be examined later. In any event, slowly and
systematically the strikes spread, as workers everywhere
demanded the same material advantages as those granted
at Ursus and Zeran.

The decisive step in this movement was only taken two
weeks later in Lublin, a town of 300,000 situated 200
kilometers (130 miles) southeast of Warsaw: on 16 July,
the railway employees took action, followed almost
instantaneously by most of the town's industries.

The first strike in 1980 occurred at the beginning of July, at the Ursus tractor factory, over an increase in the price of meat. The movement spread throughout July until, by the middle of August, it had reached the shipyards of the Baltic coast. The picture below shows the Ursus factory at a standstill during the first "Free Saturday" proclaimed by the independent union.

This time the strikers did not limit themselves to demands for meat—"We are not dogs," said one of them, "to be bribed with a bone." They presented a platform of thirty-five demands including freedom of the press, the abolition of special supply channels for the privileged, a right to the same pensions and family subsidies as the police and the army, and several other issues that were to reappear a month later in the twenty-one clause platform of the Gdansk strikers. Another element that the two events had in common was the presence of

Mieczyslaw Jagielski, deputy minister, who was urgently dispatched to Lublin, just as a month later he would negotiate with Lech Walesa in the Baltic shipyards.

But although Lublin played an important part in that turbulent summer in Poland, it had neither the influence nor the experience to become the nerve center of a national strike. This role could only be fulfilled by Gdansk, where the workers were far from forgetting the bloody conflict of 1970. At Gdansk, too, a small but highly respected group, "the Movement for Free Trade Unions," was

already at work, and conditions in general were more conducive to action on the part of the workers. Thus on 14 August 1980, when work stopped in the Lenin shipyards—ostensibly in reaction to the dismissal of Anna Walentynowicz, a dissident worker—everyone in Poland immediately understood that a critical threshold had been crossed. From now on, the escalating conflict was no longer purely social, but also political: in the Gdansk platform, point number 1 demands that workers be allowed to form a free trade union, and point 2 calls for the right to strike. For the first time, the workers were proposing to claim for themselves—permanently—the power to defend their work force. In Eastern Europe, where the ruling party professes to act on behalf of the working class, these demands were a challenge to party doctrine, undermining its legitimacy, and seemed thus

incompatible with the fundamental premise of the regime.

Since then, the Polish crisis has filled the Western press. The national British daily, *The Guardian,* was the first newspaper to proclaim in its headlines the danger of a Soviet reaction which would overthrow the balance between East and West: and the renowned *La Stampa* went so far as to bemoan the "European tragedy."

In Poland, however, the impact of the strike was by no means experienced as a "tragedy." On the contrary, in Gdansk, in Gdynia, throughout the coastal region, every day new factories joined in suppport of the shipyard workers' demands. An interfactory strike committee, the MKS, was formed, and by the side of Lech Walesa stood men such as Andrzej Gwiazda, an engineer from the Elmoi electrical equipment factory, and Bogdan Lis, a twenty-eight-year-old worker and a party member. An even younger delegate, twenty-one-year-old Bogdan Kotodziej, arrived from Gdynia. The large conference hall at the shipyards was soon filled literally to overflowing with all the elected representatives of the striking factories.

On Monday 18 August, the party leader, Edward Gierek, at last addressed the nation. He acknowledge the failures of the five-year plan, proposed new union elections, but said nothing about negotiating with the workers in Gdansk. In fact, his representative on the spot, Politburo member Tadeusz Pyka, refused to talk to the MKS, declaring such an interfactory coalition illegal, and he suggested separate negotiations with each individual factory. This was an obvious tactical ruse, designed to divide the strikers, to isolate the weakest elements and to stall

The course of the strike at the Lenin shipyard was followed with critical attention by the rest of Poland, and the Western world. Crowds began to gather outside the gates on the second day of the strike (above). The celebration of Mass in the shipyard (left, on the last day of the strike) became a regular feature.

Negotiations were started with Klemens Gniech, the shipyard director (below left). Then, on 22 August, the government, in the persons of Tadeusz Fiszbach and

Mieczyslaw Jagielski, the deputy prime minister, agreed to talk to the interfactory strike committee (MKS) (opposite page, below right).

Negotiations continued against a background of worker occupation (below), until agreement was reached on 31 August. Lech Walesa addressed the crowd from the gates for the last time (above), and the agreement was signed (above right). The shipyard gates were flung open to the crowd (right) amid scenes of jubilation (bottom right).

for time, counting on the strikers to grow weary. This attitude was a new departure for a regime that has always considered it necessary to apply global solutions to the whole of society, thereby avoiding the chaos that rules in the capitalist countries, where each economic sector or each enterprise is handled individually.

In any event, Gierek and his colleagues could not long remain inflexible, for time was not on their side. For one thing, the strike continued to spread, and now encompassed another nerve center of the coast, Szczecin, the city that counted the greatest number of victims in the riots of December 1970. Second, the ruling class itself was divided, while complaints could be heard on every side against ten years of erratic administration by Edward Gierek and his team, composed mainly of Silesians (from Poland's southern mining district).

Gierek had come to power in 1970 after fourteen years of the lackluster Gomulka administration, promising to satisfy everyone's needs and to build a "new Poland." Mocking the peasant mentality of his predecessor, who was afraid of incurring debt, Gierek sought credits in the

56

West, bought everything which came his way, and ran up debts of more than twenty billion dollars. It was due to this policy, which did not include supposedly "unprofitable" investments in infrastructure such as energy or transport, that after the artificial boom of the first years, the Polish economy entered a downward spiral. The economy of a country can never be a sphere apart, isolated from its political and social life.

And thus Gierek became more conciliatory toward the Russians than his austere predecessor Gomulka. Apparently fearful lest his rush for Western gold antagonize the U.S.S.R., he sought to offer Moscow tokens of his fidelity. In 1979, on orders from the Kremlin, he agreed to increase military expenditures (Poland spends more than 5 percent of its gross national product on armament), and then announced his unconditional support of the Soviet invasion of Afghanistan. For a country like Poland, which had so often expressed its commitment to national identity and self-respect, Gierek's servile attitude toward Brezhnev was intolerable. People even began to miss Gomulka: he at least, they said, even within the framework of "limited sovereignty," had, like the Rumanian chief Ceausescu, maintained a certain dignity.

But that was not all: with his stream of dollars, marks and francs, Edward Gierek seemed to be deluding himself that all was well. "The wealth of each citizen," he said, "contributes to the wealth of society as a whole." And no one was in a better position for self-enrichment than the members of the economic and political establishment— especially in they had no scruples. Finally, in order to safeguard their privilegs, Gierek outdid all other East European leaders in his investments in the police. He was insensitive enough to grant the police force all possible privileged treatment, and to flaunt this favoritism before the whole nation.

A single example gives a fair idea of the havoc he caused. In August, with Poland already struggling with its massive strike, the Party weekly *Polityka* was reporting on the future plans and dreams of children attending a school in Warsaw. "When I grow up, I would like to be in the police force and have a Rolls Royce," said one girl. A boy wrote: "I would like to be in the military commando and own a house and a Mercedes." *Polityka*'s purpose in publishing these statements was of course to amuse its readers and denounce the insidious influence of television films imported from the United States. But in fact these young

Poles were merely expressing aloud the secret values of their parents, which are altogether selfish, totally removed from any collective aspirations. The children's comments, all unwittingly, raise another issue: just what sort of society is it that places the police at the top of its social hierarchy?

At the Communist party headquarters, during the eventful week of 18–24 August 1980, the question of the police provoked a bitter debate. The Party finally agreed to negotiate with the strikers' interfactory committee (MKS) and dispatched two high-ranking officials, Mieczyslaw Jagielski to Gdansk and Kazimierz Barcikowski to Szczecin. But at the same time a police task force was converging on the coast to ensure order. The men had been trained at the formidable Golendzinow base, near Warsaw, the same camp which had housed the anti-strike shock troops of Marshal Pilsudski before the war. This time, even as negotiations went on, a dramatic operation—with the code name "little party"—was being prepared. Troops were to be sent by helicopter or even by sea to seize the MKS presidium at Gdansk. None of this was put into execution because one group within the Party, led by Stanislaw Kania, doubted that the repression forces were "secure" and feared that intervention on their part would only aggravate the situation. Kania was not very well known, because he operated behind the scenes, appearing very rarely in public. But for ten years he had had the task of controlling the security services and the army, as well as supervising relations with the Church. In fact, his powers were so broad that he could be considered second-in-command in the Party, and as far as the police are concerned, commander-in-chief. It was his view that prevailed on 24 August, at the plenary session of the Central Committee: Gierek remained in power but had to part with six members of the Politburo (out of eighteen),

all his Silesian friends and protégés, including the prime minister, Babiuch, and the unfortunate Pyka who had been sent to Gdansk.

From that date on, the path was at last cleared for negotiations. But the outcome remained highly uncertain. Witnesses of the deputy prime minister's arrival at the shipyards have all assured me that it was a memorable scene: *"Na Kolana! Na Kolana!"* ("On your knees! On your knees!"). No one will ever know who first cried out these words but they were echoed by thousands of voices: "Beg forgiveness, you profiteer—you've robbed us of our work and our health!" It was a moment of extreme tension, because many believed that Jagielski, even though he was protected by Lech Walesa and four workers from the security force, would have no choice but to kneel down, in a gesture of contrition. It was only by miracle that he arrived unharmed, although very pale, at the conference room. But half an hour later, Jagielski was again speaking with all the arrogance of power, as if he thought he could dupe the strikers.

Jagielski's aim, and the policy of the Party in general, was to make the MKS at Gdansk give up its plan to form an independent union and participate in the reorganization of the existing union. To show that the offer was serious, on 27 August the Party called an emergency meeting of the National Council of Trade Unions (CRZZ) in Warsaw and had them elect as chief the unionist Romuald Jankowski, who was not, contrary to tradition, a member of the leading circles of the Party. Moreover, the council decided to create its own price and wage board, announcing that from now on it would cease to be an instrument of the government and would oppose its decisions. At any other time such an organization might have meant something. But it came too late. Lech Walesa and his supporters were suspicious of everything that came from Warsaw and in any case they wanted to form their own union based on their own strike committees, independently of existing institutions.

"This is the first time we have spoken to each other for

One of the most tangible, and extraordinary, achievements of the strikes in Gdansk and Gdynia was the erection in both cities of memorials to the workers killed during the suppression of the 1970 strikes. The desire to commemorate the victims of 1970 was well established before the strikes in August. In 1978 and 1979 Walesa and Andrzej Gwiazda managed to organize gatherings before Gate No. 2 of the Lenin yard, scene of the bloodiest repression in 1970. In 1979 many participants were arrested. Walesa avoided arrest, but had

lost his job in February because of his avowed intention to have the events of 1970 properly commemorated. His resolve that 1980 would see the erection of a fitting memorial must have seemed unlikely of achievement then, but the monument became a key demand of the strikers in August 1980.

A temporary memorial was erected at Gdansk during the strike (opposite page, above left) and a committee was set up to organize the construction of a permanent monument (opposite, below). The design was exhibited at the strike headquarters (opposite, above right) and the construction carried out by volunteers from the shipyard (center). A detail of the decoration is shown at top right.

The inauguration on 16 December 1980 marked the first occasion in an Eastern European country that a memorial has been erected to workers who rebelled against the state. In the presence of high government and Church officials (above) and crowds of ordinary citizens (left), it became, however, chiefly an expression of Polish nationalism and patriotism.

63

thirty-five years," Walesa remarked in passing to Jagielski—to make clear that this was not to be the sort of negotiation that had occured in 1956 or 1970: this time, his strike committee was to be the embryo of an independent workers' movement that would not be an integral part of the system. Knowing the international contraints imposed upon Poland, however, he did not demand that the movement be turned into a political party—only that

it be legalized as a self-governing, independent union: a sort of de facto opposition to the Party, which in accordance with the Constitution would retain its role as ruler of society. It was a question of either/or, and the Polish Communist party had no choice but to sign the Gdansk agreement, which it did on 31 August.
Stanislaw Kania was to point out later with good reason that this agreement, like those concluded at the same

time at Szczecin and Jastrzebie in Silesia, had only been possible because "certain people" at the Party's political headquarters had been willing to sign. It must be added, however, that their good intentions had been prodded by the social crisis that had gripped the whole country at the end of August. Poland was on the verge of a spontaneous general strike—an event all but unprecedented in the history of the workers' movement. In every town, factories stopped work, one after the other; transport came to a standstill and slowly but surely the country shut down. Even the appeal from Cardinal Wyszynski, Primate of Poland, for moderation and a return to work, was of no avail. When the wave of strikes began to engulf Silesia, Gierek's territory, which enjoyed special concessions regarding wages and food supplies, it became evident that the regime, unable to count on support from any workers' sector, would be forced to yield before disaster overtook. For Gierek himself, this was the end: on 4 September, Kania presented him with compromising documents concerning his protégé, Maciej Szczepanski, director of the state television, notorious for his corruption. This brought on Gierek's heart attack and his departure "for reasons of health."

Poland then started off again on a new footing. A new secretary general, Kania, was hastily installed in office, and hailed by the Church as a "firm and loyal man." And Solidarity became the only union of its kind in the Soviet bloc. In September 1980 began the second chapter of what they call in Warsaw "the new Spring."

I am not among those who claim that societies of Eastern Europe are hidebound, impenetrable to new influences, so that nothing in that part of the world can possibly change. I am convinced that the process that began in Poland last summer is fundamentally unlike the situation of Hungary in 1956 or Czechoslovakia in 1968; it could, in fact, gradually reshape a regime that in its present form is unacceptable to the workers and to the greater bulk of the Polish people. Such a transition toward a pluralist system—were it to succeed—could eventually become a model for the other countries of the Soviet bloc. Little wonder, then, that the Soviets are doing everything within their power to isolate it, and of course their threats against "anti-Socialist" elements, which sometimes include the Polsih Communist party itself, place a toll on each new development in Poland. The TASS news agency accompanies each of its specious commentaries with a stamping of boots which can be heard all too clearly in Warsaw and Gdansk.

But apart from a die-hard fringe group, the Poles have long been aware that they live under a regime of "limited sovereignty" which excludes any full-fledged direct participation on the political scene. All the country's serious opposition movements, beginning with KOR (created in 1976 by Jacek Kuron and Adam Michnik), mindful of the imposed limits, have refrained from making any direct bid for power. The same is true of Lech Walesa and his companions in Solidarity, who have succeeded in enrolling more than ten million members within the space of a few months—a record envied even by the trade unions of Western Europe. They acknowledge "the leadership of our society by the Polish United Workers Party" (the Communist party) and insist that they are not concerned with politics. In actual fact they are practicing the only politics possible in the particular circumstances of their country: rather than aspire to import a parliamentary democracy from the West—a system based on a completely different notion of property—they are seeking new institutions and fighting to extend the boundaries of freedom in a society formed along particular lines and strongly "influenced" by its neighbors. All their successes to date are grounds for guarded optimism about the final result of this experiment. There is no denying the difficulties they face—the constant need to invent new solutions, day after day, week after week, while never forgetting for one instant that they are in the midst of the Soviet bloc with its unpredictable reactions.

It is worthwhile reminding ourselves, once and for all, of a fact that one is tempted to repeat over and over: the

The establishment of Solidarity as an organization rather than a mass movement began modestly, in one small room in Gdansk (below) with a crucifix, and a portrait of the Pope. It rapidly became clear that the first and most important task facing the newly formed union would be keeping up pressure on the government to carry out the measures contained in the Gdansk Agreement.

events we are witnessing are without precedent. Never before in the history of an Eastern European country, to cite one instance, has a monument been erected such as the one at Gdansk in honor of the workers who rebelled against the system in 1970; from now on, 16 December is set aside in Poland to commemorate the victims of that act of repression. Also for the first time, early in 1981 constituent congresses for the new union were held in all the large firms in Poland, with elections conducted by secret

ballot. Owing to the number of candidates and the number of voting rounds, these meetings sometimes lasted three or four days. I am told that this experiment in direct democracy has done even more than last summer's strikes to guarantee Solidarity's base among the rank and file. Those holding position of responsibility at any level know that from now on they have a regular mandate and can count on their comrades' support. For this reason, as soon as a conflict with the authorities erupts, Solidarity transfers its base of operations to the large factories, where it can be guarded by the workers.

It should be mentioned that industrialization in Poland, as throughout the Soviet bloc, is conceived primarily on the large scale, favoring gigantic installations, to the detriment of the small or medium-sized concern. But today, in a historic reversal that the founders of the Party could never have foreseen, these same mammoth industrial complexes have become Solidarity's most reliable strongholds. Beginning in the spring of 1981, the fledgling Polish labor movement, feeling less threatened, is starting to emerge from what a Polish sociologist has called its "Messianic, spontaneous phase."

It is hardly surprising that the new union was slow to get organized. During the August 1980 strike, the presidium of the MKS (local committee) at Gdansk had posted the famous slogan "Workers from all factories, unite" over the gateway to the Gdansk shipyards. But of course Lech Walesa and his companions did not know all those who were flocking to join them. Their movement sprang up spontaneously on all sides, a classic example of the "fusion group" as defined by Jean-Paul Sartre. The men

From the first, the strength of Solidarity lay in its grassroots nature, in evidence in the picture below where women workers in an electric components factory are wearing Solidarity badges. From this evolved two important Solidarity tactics: the calling for warning strikes to pressurize the government, and the withdrawal of the leadership into the factories during crises (left, the gates of the Lenin shipyard close for the start of a four-hour strike).

of them over the age of thirty—men who never experienced the war or the German occupation. They believe that the promises of their government are to be taken literally. And so they take certain rights for granted: to begin with, the right to work; but also the right to medical aid, education, everything associated with the welfare state. I was impressed by these young leaders, men such as those of Gdansk already mentioned, or Zbigniew Bujak, a twenty-six-year-old electrical worker at the

Ursus plant who became Solidarity's leader in Warsaw, or Kazimierz Slowik, a transport worker in Lodz, aged thirty. Their influence is bound to increase, so that after Solidarity's national congress, they will play an important role in the union's collective leadership.

Workers, however, are not the only group that responded to the banner at Gdansk calling for unity. A group of intellectuals in Warsaw drafted an appeal to the government during the strike, urging it to negotiate with Lech Walesa's committee (MKS). In the space of one day, the appeal was signed by sixty-four professors and writers

of Gdansk were reluctant at first to assume responsibility for a mass movement that threatened to get out of hand. They recommended that Solidarity be organized regionally, in independent units, without national leadership. But the Wroclaw delegate, Karol Modzelewski, made the shrewd observation that the authorities would find it all too easy to exploit such a division. And at the beginning of September the movement adopted his resolution for the creation of the KKP *(Krajowa Komisja Porozumiewawcza),* the National Coordination Committee, with Walesa at its head. Every week he attended meetings at presidium headquarters in the Morski Hotel in Gdansk, and sometimes in smaller towns, where they could stay closer to events and to their base. Having witnessed one of these meetings in October 1980 I can testify to the fact that the presidium took pains to respect the autonomy of each regional organization, acting more as a coordinator than a national executive organ. I was also struck by something else at this session. This new Polish trade union movement is led by a whole new generation—few

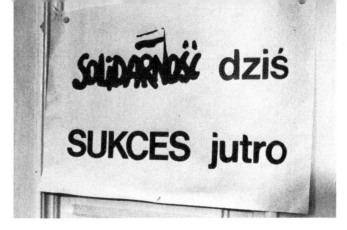

"Solidarity today, success tomorrow" (right, *on a poster at Warsaw University). The appearance in Eastern Europe of a trade union independent of government control and even negotiating as an equal partner with the government was remarkable enough. But first, Solidarity had to decide on its own internal organization. The establishment of a "National Coordination Committee" at the Gdansk headquarters* (below)

He is thus acquainted with many of the people involved in the Solidarity movement, and this proved invaluable during the early meetings between delegates who were meeting for the first time. Geremek was also of great assistance, since his international connections helped Solidarity to establish links with trade unions abroad, first of all in France and Italy. Finally, the contribution of the two economic experts, Waldemar Kuczynski and Tadeusz Kowalik, cannot be stressed enough: they provided Solidarity with essential data for drawing up a balance sheet on Gierek's administration, and they continue to analyze economic trends for the union.

The third component of Solidarity—and the most controversial—is KOR (Workers' Self-Defense Committee). KOR had the foresight to realize that the crisis in Poland would revolve around the workers. It has never been a politically homogeneous organization: its members include that doyen of Polish economists, the socialist Edward Lipinski, as well as a Catholic priest, Father Zieja, and a famous actress, Helena Mikolajska, who does not claim to represent any specific doctrinaire position. But

(including Henryk Samsonowicz, who subsequently became rector of the University of Warsaw), and was baptized the "Appeal of the Sixty-Four," although the signatures later ran into the hundreds. Two of the leaders of this campaign, Tadeusz Mazowiecki, editor-in-chief of the Catholic review *Wiez,* and Bronislaw Geremek, professor of medieval history and organizer of the "flying university" (the mobile underground teaching institution or TKN), presented their document to Walesa in Gdansk. Just as negotiations with the authorities were about to open, Walesa asked these men to remain with him as his "experts" and to recruit some other intellectuals capable of drafting the proposed agreements. This is how Walesa came to acquire his "braintrust," a group that has been so active in the leadership (KKP) of Solidarity—too active, according to complaints by some of the disgruntled rank and file.

But to my mind, these experts have in fact given Walesa valuable help, and not just because they know how to draw up documents. A former representative in the national congress, Tadeusz Mazowiecki is not only an editor but also head of the intellectual Catholic associations.

ensured that contact would be maintained between the various regions. Bottom left: *Walesa, elected as its head, is seen addressing one of the first meetings of the committee.*

Typical of the young, postwar generation who largely make up the leadership of Solidarity is twenty-six-year-old Zbigniew Bujak, from the Ursus tractor factory in Warsaw (left). *Solidarity's appeal to the* Polish working class was immediate and immense. Membership of the old government-controlled unions fell off very fast, as the membership of Solidarity reached an estimated eight million by early November—including many members of the Communist party. The scene below shows the first Solidarity demonstration, in Warsaw (Walesa, center, holding flowers, behind the banner).

since the beginning, KOR has sought to create the very bond between workers and intellectuals that is such a positive innovation in Poland's present development. KOR raised funds for victims of the 1976 repression, and at this time was also helping Lech Walesa. It was responsible for starting up a whole swarm of photocopied publications, including *Robotnik* (The Worker), which was circulated in factories and helped disseminate dissident ideas. In fact, in July 1980, during the initial phase of the "hot summer," KOR was well enough known in many factories to be the first to receive the information that "we are going on strike." It would communicate this news to the accredited correspondents in Warsaw, and from there it would reach the rest of the population over the BBC or Radio Free Europe. In mid-August, in an effort to halt this practice, the government placed Kuron, Michnik, and about ten of their colleagues under preventive arrest,

and had their arrest warrants renewed every forty-eight hours. When it came time to sign the Gdansk agreements, Walesa and his friends found themselves in an awkward position where KOR was concerned. Prime Minister Jagielski, who was negotiating with them, had already declared: "All right, I'll sign." But he had stressed that, on the subject of KOR he was not competent, the judiciary being in theory independent. Walesa and his friends, however, notably Alicja Pinkowska, a young nurse from the shipyards, outwitted him here. "All right—we'll sign," they declared, but work would only be resumed after the imprisoned members of KOR had been set free. They were released the same day.
Since then, the Polish government has understood that it can no longer arrest Kuron or Michnik, because Solidarity regards them as its advisers and an integral part of its organization even though they have no official status.

But not all dissidents are defended so staunchly. Solidarity voiced no reaction, or almost none, to the imprisonment on 22 September 1980 of Lesyek Mocyulski, the founder of an anti-Communist right-wing neo-Pilsudski type "Confederation of Independent Poland." The new Polish workers' movement withheld its support, not because it was manipulated by Jacek Kuron, but on the contrary because neither Kuron nor Solidarity wanted any part of an absurd struggle to overthrow the regime and break with the U.S.S.R. (More recently, however,

Alicja Pinkowska, a nurse at the Lenin shipyard (left) twice played an important role in the negotiations. At the beginning of the strike she played a key role in persuading the shipyard workers to remain on strike in support of the other coastal factories. Then, when members of KOR were still under arrest at the end of the negotiations, she was among those who decided that work would not recommence until the KOR members had been released.

Solidarity expressed support for the release of Mocyulski and his fellow prisoners. One of the main demands of the August 1980 strike was that no one would be imprisoned for his political views—and the government acceded to it.) More than once, moreover, the creater or of KOR has done everything in his power, working side by side with Walesa, to try and avoid strikes, first at Huta Warszawa, then in March 1981 at Radom. But in the eyes of the U.S.S.R., and to some members of the Polish Communist party, Kuron is a *bête noire* because he is a reminder to all and sundry of the powerlessness of the regime: it cannot afford to arrest this man who has the qualities of a political leader and cannot be passed off as just a trade unionist. One other reason why the Polish Communists have labeled Kuron, Michnik, and to a lesser extent Karol Modzelewski as "demons" is that all three of them emerged from the ranks of the Party itself, and all three, particularly Kuron and Michnik, have served long prison terms, in 1963 and 1968, for attempts to reform the Communist party from within. Today, the Party, with a guilty conscience where these men are concerned, is unwilling to see them circulate freely in the political

arena. Far better to brand them "anti-Socialists"—whereas in fact, if a political label had to be assigned to them, they are ideologically closer than anyone else to the Second International, and therefore quite authentic Socialists. What is really at stake in the battle between the Communist party and Solidarity is clearly not KOR and its so-called "deplorable anti-Socialist influence." To understand the stakes in this game, it is necessary to take a closer look at the party of Stanislaw Kania.

Since the signing of the Gdansk agreements, Solidarity has three times ordered warning strikes lasting between one and four hours, and on 31 March 1981 it decided to stage a general strike of unlimited duration. According to our Western standards, all these conflicts could be considered political rather than labor issues. Only once, in the case of the struggle for free Saturdays, was the dispute an economic and social one. And none of Solidarity's threatened strike actions, not even the general strike, were attempts to overthrow the authorities, but rather they sought to amputate corrupt elements in the state and regain control of their own police.

As already stated, no Eastern bloc country has invested so heavily in its police as Poland during the last ten years. The police force, though it was not used against the strikers in the "hot summer," is still in place, on call at any moment. Furthermore, the situation is quite different to that of 1956, when the new leader, Wladislaw Gomulka,

came out of prison: this time the Polish security forces are not suffering from a guilty conscience. Indeed, far from regretting its abuses of power, the police force deplores its tolerance of the various opposition groups, such as KOR. Admittedly, it is rare in history that a totalitarian regime has yielded so much ground, without making any attempt to mobilize its immense repressive machinery. According to Stanislaw Kania, as mentioned above, this machinery, except in its top echelon, is far from reliable. In August 1980, General Jaruzelski expressed the same reservations about his army, composed of draftees—who are they but the sons and brothers of strikers? Many other leaders, including for example Stefan Olszowski, an ambitious foreign minister who openly coveted the job of secretary general of the Party, voiced thier conviction that Poland had sufficient means at its disposal to restore order. They claim of course to favor reform, but not at the price of "anarchy." Their views were of course enthusiastically supported by Moscow, since Leonid Brezhnev would like nothing better than to assign the Polish Communists the task of repressing their own workers. It is not by chance that the Warsaw Pact military maneuvers coincided with the crises in Poland: the aim was obviously to encourage those in favor of repression.

So far, however, the hardliners have not prevailed, and each provocation by the police wing of the Party has been followed by a retreat, discrediting still further the Party

Solidarity's most effective tactic: the warning strike. Right: A deserted street in Gdansk in January. Far right: A tram driver wearing the Polish colors on his arm, and trams at the depot. Below, left and far right, and bottom far right: Scenes from the first warning strike in October 1980. Bottom right: The police, whose privileged status has been a special cause of dissatisfaction.

away at the concessions already won by Solidarity, and also to show that Kania and his colleagues had yielded too far, and to no purpose.

With this in mind, it is both informative and amusing to observe some of the objections to Solidarity's statutes raised by the Warsaw judge. The document signed at Gdansk, for the first time in the history of the Eastern bloc, uses the terms *pracodawcy* (employees—"recipients of work") and *pracobiorcy* (employers—"providers of work"). And the Solidarity statutes—taking as their premise this official recognition of the division of society into at least two classes whose interests are rarely reconcilable—declared that the leaders of the Party and of the state cannot belong to the same union as the workers. The Warsaw judge claimed that this amounted to discrimination against one category of citizen and therefore constituted a violation of "human rights." But in the end the threat of a general strike convinced this judge's superiors that the statutes were in order after all.

which the rebellious workers, since March 1981, have been forcing to change its ground rules. If this tendency should continue, it would mean a turning point almost as crucial as the creation of Solidarity. But rather than speculate on the future, it is more useful to review in some detail the crises that have erupted in recent months.

They invariably broke out on the eve of an important meeting of the Central Committee, and the first two clashes, in November 1980, were provoked by judicial magistrates: the first by a Warsaw judge, who on his own initiative saw fit to modify Solidarity's statutes, and the second by a prosecutor who ordered a thorough search of the union's Warsaw offices and charged two unionists with "revealing state secrets." But clearly the Polish judiciary has never been so independent as to make even the clumsiest attempt at independent interpretation of existing laws. Each of these events was a case of pseudo-legal rigging reflecting the struggle within the direction of the Party. By their legal wiles, the hardliners hoped to whittle

Apart from such pseudo-judicial crises, there was a second type, which concerned privileged local leaders, and the police in particular. The two factions of the Politburo, led by Kania and Olszowski respectively, had at least agreed from the outset on one point: the corruption in the Gierek regime had gotten out of hand. Not only did they expel Gierek and his supporters from all positions of responsibility, they also enunciated a new policy: "We aim to purge the Party of those who have dishonored it through their immoral behavior, and to defend those comrades who have been unustly slandered for abuses they did not commit."

"Poland today," a friend remarked jokingly, "is a country of thirty million private detectives and self-styled prosecutors, who are convinced that their leaders are dividing up among themselves the country's $20 billion national debt." But although he deplores this "thief-hunt," this same friend is convinced that it will not cease until the leading officials of Gierek's administration have left the scene. So far they show no signs of retiring. On the contrary, the men belonging to the state machine, feeling threatened, are closing ranks and blocking any new initiative.

Inevitably, people in many areas are refusing to take this lying down: with the aid of Solidarity, they have demanded—in Bielsko-Biala, Rzeszow, and Wloclawek—the departure of the most compromised leaders, the confiscation of villas, and the abolition of the special clinics for the police. In these struggles, moreover, the people have always been backed by Party base membership, and the government usually starts out swearing to defend its unpopular bureaucrats, then invariably gives in—of course losing face in the process. In order to win back a little of the lost ground, in February the Party

Solidarity's road to official recognition was not smooth. The first attempt failed when the judge, Kosciecwicz (left), refused to register the statutes without alterations. Walesa's reaction (right) was eloquent. Eventually, public pressure, in the form of a threatened general strike, achieved success. The placard (right) outside the court in Warsaw reads "Polish Solidarity will win"; far right, in the tram, "We demand the registration of Solidarity without modifications."

entrusted the government to a military man, General Wojciech Jaruzelski, the minister of defense. Never in Eastern Europe has a general held such a high position. But the Poles, and Solidarity in particular, welcomed him in this position. It takes at least two to have a dialogue, and until then the government had seemed without either a face or a voice. Jaruzelski, taking advantage of this good will, suggested a truce of three months without any strikes, and for better or for worse Solidarity agreed.

At this point the country seemed on the road to stability. And so, apparently to stop this process, the police wing went into action, provoking a particularly serious incident at Bydgoszcz. On 19 March, in this town of 350,000 situated halfway between Warsaw and Gdansk, the police, using their truncheons and clubs, evicted delegates of Solidarity who had come to police headquarters to discuss the problems of local farmers in the presence of the deputy prime minister, Mieczyslaw Mach. It was the first time since the creation of the independent union that the authorities, either local or central, had resorted to force. What is more, this intervention occurred barely forty-eight hours after a mass meeting at Radom, during which Lech Walesa, with the help of Jacek Kuron, had succeeded in annulling a strike called as protest against those responsible for the 1976 acts of repression. Walesa made no appeal for mercy for those officials, but instead declared: *"Dobierzemy sie do nich wszystkich"*—"We'll drive them all out!" He made this promise because General Jaruzelski had given Walesa "his word as a Polish officer" that his government would purge the security force of its most compromised elements and of those most hated by the population.

What happened at Bydgoszcz is reminiscent, on a smaller scale, of the events of 1976 in Radom. With the same display of arrogance, the police at Bydgoszcz used their truncehons on unarmed workers, of whom twenty or so, including three Solidarity representatives, had to be hospitalized. General Jaruzelski, busy accompanying Marshal Koulikov in the "Union 81" military maneuvers then

underway somewhere in Poland and East Germany, made no statement on the affair. But other officials spoke in his place. Leaders in Bydgoszcz purely and simply slandered the victims of the police brutality, claiming that they had invented their wounds or received them in car accidents caused by their own drunken driving.

Since then it has become clear that the incident was part of a vast provocation campaign directed against Solidarity as well as against those who had pledged themselves to

ship of the Polish Communist party was the problem of whether to set this force in motion. Lech Walesa and his associates could not known for certain, any more than anyone else, just what the Polish police, this state within a state, was capable of. Notwithstanding, they voted unanimously in favor of striking on 31 March 1981 and not one voice at the KKP (leadership) meeting (which in fact took place at Bydgoszcz) was raised in favor of any accommodation with the forces of repression. This does not prove that the Poles are reckless; rather, Solidarity is secure in the knowledge that it possesses the necessary strength to stand up to potential repressors.

If the special police corps are still reliable, they may be able to requisition the railway workers and the urban transport workers by declaring a state of emergency. But could they storm the shipyards, or seize Nowa Huta or Ursus or Huta Warszawa?

So Solidarity stood fast, sure of its strength, and meticulously organized the general strike of 31 March. In the West, there was some reaction of surprise and alarm at this intractability, for at first sight the new union seemed to be running enormous risks for a minor result:

reducing the high-handed activities of the police. This time, in the ongoing debate over the true value of the Polish security forces, the hardliners seemed to have the upper hand. They were preparing to show that their police were capable not only of battering isolated delegates but also of breaking up a general strike. At Warsaw there was talk of the imminent declaration of a state of siege—with the inevitable blood bath that would follow. The whole world held its breath during this test of strength, the most serious since the previous August.

Not one of Solidarity's leaders or counselors, whether moderate or radical, young or old, was unaware that Poland still possesses an overgrown instrument of repression, and that the debate that was tearing apart the leader-

A reflection of tension within the Polish government, and also of the growing power of Solidarity, was the case of Narodniak and Sapels, arrested in November and accused of revealing state secrets. Negotiations between the government and Solidarity, under threat of strike, resulted in their release. Left: A jubilant Jan Narodniak after he had been set free.

One of the main objections of ordinary Poles was to the degree of corruption among their rulers, and the luxurious life style they enjoyed at a time of economic hardship. Right: A farmer stands by the fence surrounding the Arlancow government resort near Ustrzyki Dolme. This fenced-off territory, reserved for the enjoyment of government officials, sparked off the strikes in the region in early 1981.

The demand for an independent union was rapidly taken up by Poland's private farmers (below, a farmer ploughing near Lublin). The private produce sold at markets like the one at bottom right plays a vital part in Poland's food supply. This fact ensured that, despite official reluctance, the new union, led by twenty-three-year-old Jan Kulaj (right) was eventually authorized. Far right: Farmers outside the tribunal in Warsaw.

the mere punishment of a few policemen in a country town. But there was much more at stake in this confrontation than an isolated case of violence: it was vital to demonstrate, once and for all, that the various schemes of repression within the country, devised in Moscow and in one sector of the Polish Communist party, had no solid foundations. After four days fraught with tension, the truth finally emerged: the "hard heads" of the Party, as Olszowski describes himself, clashed with their own colleagues, the huge majority of Communists, who were convinced that Poland would not survive the general strike. The hardliners, forced to show their hands, found themselves morally and politically isolated, and for a time at least, completely powerless. During a dramatic meeting of the Communist party's Central Committee on 29 March, almost all the speakers virtually denounced them as responsible not only for the Bydgoszcz incident but also for the workers' persistent and justified distrust of the existing regime. The resignations of Olszowski and two of his associates were admittedly refused—in order to

76

avoid upsetting Brezhnev still further—but their political disgrace would seem to mark a turning point in the history of the Polish Communists.

Thanks to this purge, the general strike was avoided and, more important still, the threat of violence was removed. The confrontation that took place in March 1981 therefore constitutes an important date in Poland's "self-controlled revolution," the more so because its principal protagonists—Lech Walesa's workers' movement on the one hand, the Polish Communist party on the other—were forced to draw a lesson from this encounter. It is impossible to remain indefinitely "with one foot over the precipice," to use Lech Walesa's own words. In order to avoid the repetition of such situations in the future, both sides have felt the need to put their respective houses in order; whence the importance of the congresses that the Polish Communist party and Solidarity both organized at the same time, the first in July, the second in August 1981.

Solidarity clearly wishes to remain a union and nothing more than a union. It has no desire to play the role of coadministrator in the factories and even less so in the country's institutions. But it does have views on what should happen in all firms as well as in the municipal and district councils. It maintains that leaders on all levels should be elected and responsible to the electorate. This would entail the reintroduction of councils in the firms, which would recruit directors by open competition. It would also mean organs of self-government in the various towns, regions, and districts. Life would be a great deal easier for the leaders of Solidarity if the problems of the work force could be discussed in democratic assemblies —and this is the goal of Walesa and his associates. Without this change, they will be unable to improve their own internal democracy.

In this program, for reasons that are clear, the Polish Communist party is not mentioned. But contrary to the claims of certain critics, the aim of Solidarity is not to eliminate this party from democratic competition, but to see it actively involved in this process, even wishing it a

chance of success. Thus, in a sense we are back at square
one: can Stanislaw Kania's party adapt itself to the re-
quirements of the new situation?

In order to explain the skepticism about the possibility
of "improving the Communist party" in Poland, we
must return, not to the abortive "revisionist" attempts
of 1956, but directly to the sad events of March 1968. At
this time, the police wing of the Party, taking advantage
of a student dispute arising from the Prague Spring,
succeeded in imposing on the Party ensemble a repressive

anti-intellectual and anti-Semitic line. Now, a Communist party may commit innumerable tactical or strategic
errors and get away with it, but it cannot become racist
without degrading itself profoundly, without "changing
in nature." For when it embarks on such a line of policy,
its best elements leave, giving way to the mediocre and
the unscrupulous social climbers. And that is precisely
what happened in Poland in 1968.

To take a single example: when one of the best-known
Poles in the international field, Adam Rapacki, minister

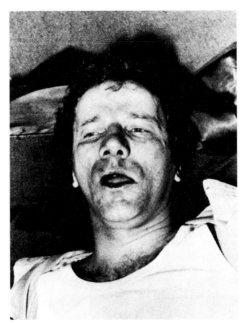
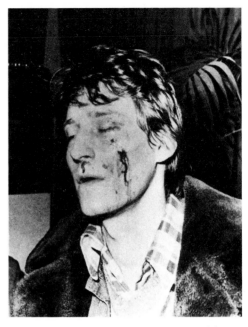

for foreign affairs, was presented with the list of Jews to be expelled from his ministry, he added his own name with his own hand, and departed. Many others, not so well-known, retired in a similar way, entirely renouncing their roles in the state and the Party. Those who replaced them, recruited among the perpetrators of a real cultural pogrom, were of an intellectual and moral standard too low to inspire the least confidence in the population or even in the members of the Communist party, who from that moment ceased to take an interest in politics and Party affairs. The gap between the machinery of power, which was sinking deeper into corruption, and the rest of society had not ceased to widen, even in the heart of the Party.

For this reason, after the explosion of the summer of 1980, all those who desired a new beginning and "a reconciliation between Poles" asked the Party for an explanation of the 1968 affair and requested that at least its most compromised members be discharged. At the start of the academy year 1980–1981, this question began to be discussed in all the Polish universities, at the Academy of Science, at the writers' and journalists' congresses. In Warsaw, the University Senate set up an inquiry commission, chaired by Professor Klemens Szaniawski, to find out how, on 22 March 1968, at the mere order of a few illiterate policemen, it had been possible to exclude six of the best professors from teaching, with Leszek Kolakowski, Bronislaw Baczko, and Wlodzimierz Brus at the top of the list. In a resolution taken on 12 November last year, the commission stigmatized the authorities and the University Senate of the time, offering apologies in their

name to the victims. But Solidarity asked for more: why leave out all the teachers and students who had been beaten up, sentenced to terms of imprisonment, or ejected from the University? And shouldn't the anti-Semites who were now replacing them, mainly in the Ministry of Security, be denounced as well?

Amid all this, on 8 March 1981, at a grand assembly at the University of Warsaw, chaired by the new rector, Henryk Samsonowicz, and addressed by Zbigniew Bujak, the district president of Solidarity, the question of Jacek Kuron and Adam Michnik, victims of the events of thirteen years ago, was discussed. But not far away, the so-called Grunwald Patriotic Association had succeeded in assembling four hundred anti-Semites to denounce those of Jewish origin who were occupying posts of responsibility in Solidarity. Furthermore, while this "sordid anti-Semitic demonstration"—to quote the headlines of *Unità*, the mouthpiece of the Italian Communist party —aroused only disgust abroad, at Warsaw, on the contrary, it received favorable reports from the official news agency, PAP. Several weeks later, the Grunwald Patriotic Association was duly legalized, as a useful public socio-cultural organization, and from then on it began to publish a weekly paper, *Reality,* printing 150,000 copies. When Stefan Olszowski was questioned on the subject, he had nothing but words of encouragement for this "anti-Zionist" organization, stating that as far as anti-Semitism was concerned, he was satisfied with the resolutions of the Fifth Congress of the Party in 1969, the era of the "white pogrom."

Resistence to democratization in the Polish Communist

party does not, therefore, simply stem from a corrupt minority left over from Gierek's time. Its roots lie in an ideological perversion that goes far deeper than that and is well illustrated by the behavior of Olszowski himself and other "hardliners" of the police division. But no party can govern opposed by all the workers (united in Solidarity), all farmers (who are members of Rural Solidarity), and in addition, all the intellectuals, who believe that the anti-Semitic policies of 1968 tarnished the image of Poland in the eyes of the rest of the world. Stanislaw Kania did not need to be a political genius to realize that he must find some kind of policy line somewhere and that the Party could not extricate itself by turning everyone against it. So, in contrast with his predecessors at the secretariat general, he did not hesitate to seek contact with the militants, above all in the factories, and they made no attempt to hide their hostility towards all the leaders of the Party.

"It is not easy to be secretary of the Party just now," he admitted sincerely and frankly at the beginning of April 1981 during a meeting with Communists from the Gdansk shipyards.

For the Party, in one sense, no crisis that occurred in the past remotely resembles that of today, because those who were discontent before had no opportunity to unite as today's workers are doing in Solidarity, and by creating their own horizontal structures, independent of the vertical mechanisms of the Communist party. The Communist party, in fact, modeled on the state and the army, is strictly hierarchical. But revolts may break out within it, just as they may break out in society. And since last winter, that is precisely what is happening.

It is well known that in the countries of the Eastern bloc, membership in the Communist party provides career opportunities. However, all members of the Party do not automatically become big shots; some remain in the factories or in small administrational jobs, gaining little from their membership cards. These ordinary members have known for a long time that things are going badly in Poland, and some of them have even tried to sound the alarm. But in the Party, their opinions hardly counted for more than those of an "ordinary" citizen of the state. No one would listen. However, when tongues finally loosened after the creation of Solidarity, the worker members of the Communist party were accused by their fellow workers of the misdeeds of the party in power, just as if they had a voice in its decisions. It is not therefore surprising that, caught between two fires, some (more than 250,000) simply handed in their cards, while others

began to gather independently, determined this time to make themselves heard at the highest Party level, not even hesitating in front of Kania himself to denounce the "red bourgeoisie." (A report including that very expression is to be found in the ultra-official journal *Polityka*.) During the night of 29 to 30 April, a new plenary meeting of the Central Committee—the seventh since the events of the summer of 1980—decided on 14 July 1981 as the date for the extraordinary congress of the Polish Communist party. The congress deserved this title, not only because the usual time limits were not to be respected, but principally because this time round, the 1,700 delegates would be elected democratically by secret ballot and with no restriction of candidates. And this is not the only new feature of Kania's plans: he has proposed an internal system that will allow the militants to check all the civil servants, by means of their elected representatives, a procedure that constitutes a complete reversal of the system that has hitherto existed. But better still, the contracts of these civil servants, including those at a very high level, should be limited to a certain period of time (probably three years) and it should no longer be possible to hold several positions of responsibility at once. For a party which dates back over a long period, that still retains the traces of the vile purge of 1968 and bears the marks of the "Gierek" decade of corruption, this project seemed unhoped-for. It is indeed a great victory for Solidarity, which by its very existence and by its democratic example has influenced the ruling party, forcing it to change under threat of disintegration. Admittedly, the innovations due to take place in the Polish Communist party are still in the planning stage and cannot yet be transformed into facts without very great changes in the Party and state machinery. But the mere possibility of change allows Solidarity to define its own role more clearly, aware as it is that its own conduct depends to a great extent on the conduct of its official negotiators. But time is of the essence in Poland, because an economic catastrophe is threatening the whole world and solutions to this crisis are hardly likely to present themselves at the congresses of either side.

For the second year in succession, the Polish national income is decreasing; according to estimates made by experts, this decline threatens to last until 1985, for time is required to set the "runaway train" of the economy on a track that will lead it in the right direction.

In order to achieve this it would be necessary to reduce the number of firms consuming too many vital raw

The constant threat of military intervention to put an end to the developments in Poland was underlined by the Soyuz 81 *Warsaw Pact maneuvers* (right) *held in Poland in March involving troops from the U.S.S.R., East Germany, and Czechoslovakia, in addition to Poland. In a picture of some symbolic content, General Jaruzelski is caught* (below) *between, on the right, the East German General Hoffman, and on the left, the Russian General Kulikov, during the maneuvers.*

materials and to develop those that export, bringing in strong currency. In the meantime, moreover, Poland will have to execute this delicate operation by keeping the present economic machinery going and thereby accumulating more debts in dollars. According to Solidarity, $ 6 to 7 billion in extra credits would be required to meet the non-transferable pay dates and to lay in supplies from the Western market. Now, although the Western governments, from the United States to France, are making a

concerted effort to help Poland, above all with foodstuffs, on the private bank exchange the country is regarded as more or less bankrupt. For Poland, the time of easy credits has come to an end, and it is now experiencing difficulty in buying the bare essentials; hence the cruel lack of spare parts and basic materials for its industries which are half paralyzed and carry on only in fits and starts.

Putting agriculture back into shape is not much easier, because building up livestock also takes time. In spite of an increase in the price of agricultural products bought by the state, it is not certain that the small farmers are

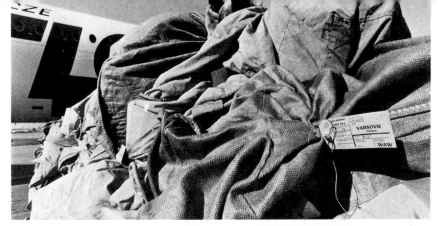

Poland's food supply had become so precarious by the spring that rationing of meat and sugar was introduced. Right: Milk and medicine flown in from the West to alleviate the shortages. Below: A queue outside a butcher's shop in Warsaw, on the day before meat rationing was introduced.

sufficiently "stimulated" to supply the market as it really needs to be. Steps taken so far have only served to aggravate the pressure of inflation, which is affecting the lives of everyone. Lucid but sad discussions of this are now to be heard everywhere, and may even be read in the official press as well as in that of Solidarity.

By the end of Spring 1981, Poland had beaten all European records for meetings, elections, and talks with leaders. In theory, two or three months should have sufficed for Poland to give exact shape to the "new beginning" that it has been formulating since the Gdansk agreements of last August. But the new campaign in the Communist party and Solidarity means postponing the planned drastic anti-inflation measures, and in the meantime increasing poverty is causing both spontaneous and manipulated reactions of ill-feeling in certain sectors of the population. In April, this erupted in attacks on police commisariats in two areas at least, Otwock near Warsaw and Kuczborg in the southwest. On each occasion, the leaders of Solidarity intervened to restore order.

The militia, aware of the open animosity of the great majority of the population, is either threatening strike action in certain areas—in Gdansk, for example—or it is resorting to force to deal with the slightest offense. The government is talking about an increase in the crime rate, but without giving precise details. The general climate has been aggravated by a drop in the production of cigarettes (12.4 percent below last year's), which have now become almost unobtainable; according to the Warsaw press, this is causing anger among smokers and sometimes, pillaging.

Ever since August 1980, there has been talk of a Soviet intervention. Most Western political scientists are of the opinion that, since the signing of the Gdansk agreements, the Polish "innovation" has been "unacceptable" to Leonid Brezhnev, who, not being a man of political subtleties, would sooner or later send his tanks to Warsaw. According to the former director of the National Security Council, Zbigniew Brzezinski, the Russians were about to intervene in Poland on 8 or 9 December last year, but an active step on the part of Carter's government dissuaded them.

One kilogram per adult per month was the amount allocated, when ration cards for sugar (left) were issued, starting in February 1981. Lengthy queues for scarce goods had long been a feature of Polish shopping (below, queuing for fruit on Dluga Street, Gdansk) but rationing had now become the only means of ensuring fair distribution of essential foodstuffs.

In March 1981, there was a new alert when the "Sojuz 81" maneuvers of the Warsaw Pact troops began, and this time it was Reagan's administration which put Moscow on its guard and actually sent U.S. Air Force observation equipment into the area. Since then, there has been less talk about Soviet military preparations, but it would be a mistake to forget that the U.S.S.R. already has troops in Poland, and that military intervention in this country poses infinitely fewer "technical" problems than it did in Czechoslovakia in 1968. It may well be that for Leonid Brezhnev, the changes currently being wrought in the Polish Communist party—and in the relation between this party and Solidarity—are the straw that will break the camel's back.

My Polish friends, in Warsaw and afterward in Paris, always assured me that excessive alarmism about the U.S.S.R.'s intentions would not help their cause. By continually crying wolf, people are preparing international opinion to accept the Soviet "coup" and there is a risk of adding coals to the fire of those who wished to obstruct the process that started with the Gdansk agreements. It is certain, on the other hand, that with today's international economic situation, the U.S.S.R. would pay a far higher price to invade Poland than it did for Czechoslovakia or Afghanistan. Moreover, it is hard to see how the Russians would run this country, with almost no support on the spot, unless they governed it from Moscow, returning to the situation at the time of the czars....

MICHAEL DOBBS

Lech Walesa: Symbol of the Polish August

Each great revolution produces a symbol. The character of the man thrown up by the rush of events says much about the nature of the revolution. The French Revolution produced the fiery oratory of Robespierre; the Russian Revolution the burning determination of Lenin. Mahatma Gandhi, frail and ascetic, personified India's non-violent revolt against the British Raj. In 1968 the world associated Czechoslovakia's Prague Spring with the wistful smile of Alexander Dubcek; full of hope, but finally too weak to resist the might of Soviet tanks.

The Polish August of 1980 produced Lech Walesa. He made no claims to being a profound thinker or a great spiritual leader. Neither is he a military genius or even a politician. At the time of his sudden emergence, he had never been outside Poland nor read a single book. Like the men he led, he is a true child of Communist Poland and embodies its ironies and contradictions. He is deeply Catholic, but clings to rudimentary socialist ideals. He is intensely patriotic. He is a realistic romantic who learned

early how to control his anger against injustice and double-talk. He is the opposite of an ideologue—a man of simple tastes guided by experience and instincts rather than by ideas.

The rise of Lech Walesa from unemployed electrician to international media celebrity has few parallels in modern history. In July 1980, when the first sporadic strikes broke out in Poland over increases in the price of food, he was an unsung dissident harassed by the authorities for his illegal union activity. Abroad, nobody had heard of him—and even within Poland, he was known only to the police and a handful of political activists in the Gdansk region. When not in prison on trumped-up charges, he lived in a mean two-room apartment with his wife and six children. In the space of a few months, his name (pronounced VAH-WEHN-SAH) had become a household world. His walrus moustache and impish grin stared from television screens and the covers of news magazines. His exploits were discussed in the highest political councils of the world—from the Kremlin to the White House to NATO headquarters in Brussels. He negotiated with Communist party leaders on equal terms and went to Rome for a private audience with Pope John Paul II, his fellow-countryman. His every move, whether eating breakfast or attending mass, was watched and chronicled by hundreds of journalists and photographers.

Small wonder then that, at one point, he himself asked in jest: "Who is this fellow on account of whom soldiers are not allowed to take their boots off even when they sleep?"

I first met Lech Walesa in the large committee room at the Lenin shipyard in Gdansk. It was Friday 15 August 1980, the second day of the strike at the shipyard—and I was the first Western journalist to be allowed to attend the negotiations between workers and management. The decision to admit me after I turned up at the shipyard gate with photographer Chris Niedenthal was taken by Walesa himself. It marked him apart from other strike leaders. During previous strikes in other parts of the country, workers had refused to talk to foreign correspon-

dents. The negotiations took place behind barred gates and no outsiders were admitted. Walesa, by contrast, was quick to grasp the value of publicity in the world news media. Of course, by the time the Gdansk strike ended seventeen days later, it had become a media event. But that first Friday, when I tried to take photographs of the strike, workers protested violently for fear they might be recognized and later harassed.

Seated across the negotiating table from me was a shortish man, about five foot seven, in a shabby dark suit and an open-neck shirt. Apart from the now famous moustache, the first things I noticed about him were his quick, darting eyes and the voice which had a kind of rasping, cheeky quality. There was an unmistakable authority to him. By the force of his personality, he was shaping the course of events. At that stage, the government was still refusing to talk with the strikers. The talks were being conducted by the shipyard director, Klemens Gniech, a liberal-minded man who later showed considerable sympathy for the strikers and their grievances. Looking grim and

tight-lipped, he did is his best to argue the authorities' case. But it was Walesa who dictated the pace of the negotiations, playing his hand with the skill of a poker buff. It was not long before Walesa insisted on the two cardinal principles that were later to emerge as the hallmarks of the independent trade union Solidarity. The first was his determination that this time the authorities would be forced to give cast-iron guarantees never to repeat the mistakes and repressive policies of the past. The second, related principle was that the workers realize the overriding importance of maintaining their unity in the face of official attempts to divide them.

Fired from the shipyard because of overzealous union activity in 1976, Walesa reappeared there on the morning of Thursday 14 August 1980 by the simple method of climbing over the perimeter wall. Two thousand workers (out of a work force of 16,000) had downed tools over the dismissal of an elderly woman crane operator, Anna Walentynowicz. Like Walesa, Mrs. Walentynowicz was a founder member of the underground Baltic Free Trade

The extensive documentation of the August strike at Gdansk, and the subsequent development of Solidarity, was largely due to the personal insistence of Lech Walesa, seen here (below left) in the Lenin shipyard, that the news media should be allowed virtually unrestricted access. One of the first pictures of the strike, taken on the second day (left) shows workers gathering in the yard.

"La Pasionaria" of Poland, as she has been called, Anna Walentynowicz (below) had a long record of political activity before her dismissal from the Lenin shipyard sparked off the strike there in August 1980. Neither her reinstatement nor the offer of a large pay rise, however, were sufficient to end the strike; the occupation of the shipyard continued (below right) as the idea of interindustry solidarity was born.

Union. Because of police harassment, the union itself never gained much influence at the shipyard—but there was a mood of smoldering rage against steadily worsening living conditions, economic mismanagement, and political repression. Mrs. Walentynowicz's case brought these resentments to the surface, but the workers lacked any organized channels for expressing them.

By the time Walesa arrived on the scene, the protests appeared to be on the verge of petering out. Without making any specific promises, one of the managers had assured the workers that their grievances would be investigated. A mass meeting was already breaking up. In the absence of anyone else, Walesa seized the leadership of the strike. Turning toward the manager, he yelled: "We don't believe your lies. We're not going to allow ourselves to be cheated again. Until you give us firm guarantees, we'll stage an occupation strike."

It was a momentous speech. Several shipyard workers told me later that, had Walesa not been there, the strike would undoubtedly have collapsed. As it was, it spread to the entire shipyard. What is more, it quickly became clear that what Walesa meant by "firm guarantees" was the creation of a fully independent, legally recognized trade union in place of the old Communist-dominated puppet organization.

Walesa demonstrated, on the second day of the strike, his instinct for workers' solidarity at all costs. The negotiations revolved largely around two issues: Mrs. Walentynowicz's reinstatement and a pay increase of 2,000 zloties ($ 66) a month for all workers. The demand, inserted by Walesa, for free trade unions was a subsidiary one which at the time appeared unrealizable in practice. Playing his cards skilfully, Gniech offered the strikers a deal granting differential pay raises to different groups of workers. As no doubt was the intention, this move split the strike committee. The representatives of those workers that stood to gain the largest increase were inclined to accept the offer. Other delegates started haggling, pushing forward their own factional interests. The issue of principle involved in Mrs. Walentynowicz's dismissal was all but

As the newly elected members of the strike committee argued over their demands in exhausting sessions (below right), the position of Lech Walesa as the leader of the strike became indisputable. His presence became an integral part of the scene at Gdansk, whether at an informal gathering for collective prayer (below left) or, together with his bodyguard, making a characteristic gesture of jubilation (right).

A new feature of the negotiations at Gdansk was the way the striking workers were kept continually informed of the progress of the negotiations. Walesa is seen (far right) during a pause, passing on information on the progress of the discussion to those waiting outside.

forgotten. As one disgruntled worker sitting next to me remarked: "We're like a pack of hungry dogs who've just been thrown a bone and are tearing ourselves apart."

At this point, Walesa's position did not seem all that strong. The strike committee was divided. Many delegates, feeling unsure of themselves, were reluctant to prolong the occupation of the shipyard into a third day. I could see the look of greed in some workers' eyes as they thought about the offer of 2,000 zloties—a hitherto unbelievable increase. Such was the mood of mutual suspicion, encouraged as a matter of policy by the authorities, that one worker confided to me: "We don't even trust our colleagues in the next department."

When the negoiations resumed after a short interval, Walesa immediately took the initiative. He insisted that Gniech reply to the workers' demands one by one, saving the divisive issue of the pay increase until the end. First, as a precondition for ending the strike, he demanded a written guarantee that Mrs. Walentynowicz be reinstated. "Otherwise," he threatened, "we break off these talks right now." There was a hush as everybody in the room wondered whether this was just a bluff. Then, from outside came a resounding cheer from thousands of workers listening to a relay of the negotiations by loudspeaker. The pressure was now on Gniech and he reluctantly agreed to the demand as "a gesture of goodwill."

Finally, the issue of pay was raised. The director again offered split increases, but was cut short by Walesa who said brusquely: "We all want these same increase, it's either two thousand for everybody or nothing." Once again there was a moment of stillness as his words were relayed outside. Then another deafening cheer. The idea of workers' solidarity had taken hold. The next crucial moment came on the third day of the strike, Saturday, when the shipyard delegates reached agreement with the management on generous terms for going back to work. All

Overleaf: *"Workers of all factories unite!"* Under the banner with this inscription, Lech Walesa, holding the pen used to sign the Gdansk Agreement in his right hand, announces the end of the strike to the crowd waiting outside, from the gates of the shipyard, amid flowers, national flags, and religious images.

workers were to receive a 15,000 zloty yearly increase—not as much as they had demanded, but more than any other group of strikers had won. In addition, there were guarantees of reinstatement for dismissed workers and security for all strikers. Walesa proclaimed "victory" and recommended that the occupation of the shipyard be called off.

This decision dismayed other workers in Gdansk. The strike at the Lenin shipyard had triggered off similar protests in other plants. Now, without the industrial muscle of the 16,000 shipyard workers, they feared their own bargaining power would be much reduced. As a leader of the striking busmen told Walesa: "If you abandon us, we'll be lost. Buses can't face tanks." Walesa was also attacked by some of the shipyard workers. At the mass meeting, a young girl yelled out that Walesa had betrayed strikers elsewhere by accepting the management offer. He then abruptly changed course. Almost hoarse after three days

Indefatigable energy and the ability to communicate successfully from shopfloor to government have meant that Walesa has become the real leader, and in no way a figurehead, of Solidarity. He is seen here (right) speaking at the Ursus tractor factory during a warning strike, carried aloft at Cracow (below), and (bottom), in contrasting postures, first addressing miners at Walbrzych, second looking more respectable and less at ease, speaking at the Solidarity gala in Warsaw.

what would happen to other workers if the shipyard called off its strike. In the end, what Walesa started became great national resurgence, a movement for the renovation of an entire inefficient system."

In order to understand why Walesa acted the way he did, it is necessary to know sommething of Poland's postwar history with its recurring cycles of rising hopes and bitter disappointments. Perrphaps more than any other revolutionary figure, Walesa is a product of his time. The essential clue to his actions lies in his past.

He was born, the son of a village carpenter, on 29 September 1943. His birthplace, the village of Popov, lies in the valley of the Vistula ("the Queen of Polish rivers") as it winds its way north from Warsaw to the Baltic coast near Gdansk. The nearest town of any size is Lipno where Lech went to technical school.

In 1943, Poland had been under Nazi occupation for four

of constant talking, he reversed himself: "What am I saying? These factories came out with us and therefore we must stay out with them. The fact that we've won doesn't mean they have won. We don't have the right to leave them alone. We've got to continue a solidarity strike until victory for everyone".

It was this speech of Walesa's that effectively turned a localized shipyard dispute into a nationwide protest. Eventually the protest became a revolution that the authorities found impossible to resist. The next day, workers at 24 factories in the Gdansk region voted to form a unified strike committee with sole powers of negotiation with the authorities. Over the following weeks, this committee grew and grew until it represented workers throughout Poland, eventually transforming itself into the independent Solidarity trade union.

As one of the shipyard delegates remarked: "This was where Walesa demonstrated his greatness. He did not think just in terms of the benefits to be gained by workers at just one shipyard—but of all Polish workers and indeed of all Polish society. He was worried by the problem of

94

Whether addressing journalists at the first Solidarity press conference (left) *or tram drivers at the Warsaw depot during a warning strike* (below right), *the pace has been unremitting for the best part of a year. Despite occasional catnaps en route the strain is considerable.* Bottom: *An exhausted Walesa during the Bydgoszcz crisis.*

years. Hitler considered the Poles an inferior race and was bent on their extermination in order to create *Lebensraum* (living space) for the Germans. Like countless other Poles, Lech's father was taken off to a concentration camp soon after the birth of his son. He died, as a result of the treatment he received, two years later. Lech's mother was left to bring up the family of seven children and look after a small seven-acre farm. Poland was in ruins after the war and it was difficult to make ends meet. In 1946, she was married again—to her brother-in-law Stanislaw, who became Lech's second father. His real father he had hardly seen, and knew of him only from his mother's stories. Walesa has a picture of himself, aged seven or eight, at his village school. His hair is shorn and, like the other children, he is dressed in outsize trousers and shirt, hand-me-downs from his elder brothers. The group looks like a crowd of urchins sitting at the feet of a stern teacher. According to his own account, Lech did not shine at any particular subject but was interested in history. He played with toy soldiers and wanted to be a pilot when he grew up. He noticed quite early that he had an ability to lead

95

Scene of some of the most dramatic recent events in Poland, the city of Gdansk (formerly Danzig) has played a crucial role in Polish history. The most important port in Poland by the sixteenth century, it lost contact with Poland after the first partition in 1772, when it became entirely surrounded by Prussian territory. The second partition of 1793 made Gdansk offi-

cially a part of Prussia, and so it remained until Poland was reestablished.

Gdansk, now a predominantly German town, became a Free City under Polish protection in 1919: an uneasy arrangement, which resulted in the city becoming the direct cause of the outbreak of World War II. The Pol-

96

ish refusal to return Gdansk to Germany was answered by invasion, and the first shot of the war was fired off Gdansk by the battlecruiser "Schleswig Holstein" on 1 September 1939.
Reintegrated with Poland at the end of the war, the old town had been almost completely destroyed. The views of the cathedral and old town (left), the Town

Hall (center) and the old river front (above) demonstrate the skill with which it was reconstructed, following old plans and illustrations. Now again one of Poland's most important ports, it is also one of the centers of the shipbuilding industry (top: the Lenin shipyard).

Right from childhood, people always
seem to have been interested in
what I say and think.
They've always followed me.

Lech Walesa

and influence his schoolmates. "Right from childhood, people always seem to have been interested in what I say and think. They've always followed me," he recalled later. Shocked by the way he expressed his views so forcefully, a priest warned him that he would end up "in prison."

Lech received a religious upbringing. His mother was a firm believer and, apart from two years in his late teens, he regularly attended church. Once he became famous, one of the things that most angered him was the suggestion that he flaunted his Catholicism for political motives. Without religious faith, he said, it would have been impossible to have persevered through years of repression. He later remembered a fit of conscience that seized him after getting drunk over a girl. "It was cold and I was tired and I looked for some sort of shelter. There was nothing nearby except a church, so I went in. I sat in a pew. It was warm and I felt so good that from that moment I ceased being a layabout."

Belief in the Catholic church provided an alternative to belief in Communism. Like many other Poles, he regarded the Church as the true protector of the Polish

nation. It was a symbol of struggle, the one national institution that refused to compromise in the face of outside attacks. He insisted: "If it hadn't been for the Church, none of this would have happened. Apart from anything else, I wouldn't be what I am."

The postwar years saw a social revolution in Poland. It was expressed partly through migration; from the eastern territories annexed by the Soviet Union after World War II to the new lands in the west acquired from Germany, from the countryside to the town, from poverty-stricken Poland itself to affluent America and Western Europe. The Walesa family was no exception. In 1973, Lech's mother and stepfather emigrated to the United States. His mother died in a car crash and Stanislaw settled down in New Jersey, taking a job as a lumberjack. Several times he suggested that his stepson should come and join him, but Lech disapproved of what he regarded as a "capitalist existence."

After three years in secondary school and completion of national service (he reached the rank of corporal), Lech began work as an electrician near his home village. He moved to Gdansk in 1966. His main concern was to find a job, but he no doubt wanted to broaden his outlook as well. Formerly the free town of Danzig, Gdansk is one

The happy couple, 1969. This rather stiffly posed studio photograph reveals little of the mixture of impudence and authority which Walesa has made his trademark during the last year. Danuta though, does seem to radiate a serene determination which must have stood her in good stead during the ups and downs of her husband's career.

Stages in the life of a trade union leader: opposite page, left, *the young Lech Walesa (back row, second from the right) photographed on a school outing in the 1950s. Corporal Walesa* (far left), *doing his national service, presenting an image of soldierly smartness somewhat at variance with the union agitator and labor leader who was to head Eastern Europe's first non-government-approved union.*
At left, a rare informal shot of the young Lech Walesa (embracing friend) in Warsaw, in the early 1960s.

of the most cosmopolitan of Polish cities. The influx of immigrants following the expulsion of the German population gives it an air of dynamism and excitement. Thanks to its history as a prosperous medieval seaport, and its position on the Baltic, it is also open to outside influences.

In Gdansk, he found work as an electrician at the Lenin shipyard. In 1969 he married a pretty florist six years younger than himself called Miroslawa. Walesa preferred the name Danuta—so it stuck. Before their marriage, they courted each other for a year, but she recalls that he never brought her any flowers: "He thinks words are enough."

A turning point in Walesa's life came in December 1970 when workers in Gdansk and other cities along the Baltic coast rioted against increases in the price of food. It was a spontaneous explosion of anger. Already politically active, the 27-year-old Walesa was elected to the strike committee at the Lenin shipyard—but there was not much either he or other strike leaders could do to control the workers' rage. After the authorities refused to talk to them, they took to the streets, attacking militiamen and burning Communist party buildings. The riots were brutally suppressed by the security services and dozens of workers were killed. (No one knows the exact figure.) This tragic experience was crucial in shaping the outlook of Walesa and his fellow strike leaders ten years later. During the shipyard strike, Walesa referred time and again to the lessons of 1970. It was a terrible mistake, he insisted, for workers to challenge the police in the streets. Instead they should simply occupy their factories and wait patiently until the authorities were ready to negotiate. Passive resistance—disciplined, good-humored, and on a massive scale—was the most effective weapon of all. Ironically, the strategy of the peaceful "occupation strike" (sometimes called "the Polish strike") was devised by Polish communists in the 1920s in their struggle against the capitalist classes. In 1980, it was turned against the people who invented it.

One result of the coastal riots was that Walesa gained a sense of political tactics and the necessity of leadership. Arousing people's anger was not enough. Crowds, he believed, had to be guided and controlled by wise men. Otherwise they degenerated into mobs: spontaneous yes, democratic possibly, but ultimately self-destructive. He also understood the value of patience. As he liked to remind himself: "A wall cannot be demolished with butts of the head. We must move slowly, step by step, otherwise the wall remains untouched and we break our heads."

In a revealing interview with the Italian journalist Oriana Fallaci, he explained: "When a man accumulates as much anger as I have accumulated over so many years, he learns

Two holiday snapshots, from Sopot, (left) in 1974, and (below) 1976, serve as reminders that there was some time for relaxation in the 1970s. The initial promise of the Gierek regime waned, however, and Walesa, accused of "disorderly conduct" and sacked in 1976, began his clandestine fight for free trade unions.

then were almost identical to those made by his successors in 1980 and by Gomulka when he came to power in 1956. He blamed the former regime for "grave errors" and "distortions of Socialism." The Communist party, he insisted, would reform itself—in order to ensure that the mistakes of the past were never repeated.

For a time, life did improve. Walesa took advantage of the new, more relaxed political climate to work within the official trade unions. The unions were given greater independence and became more assertive in defending workers' interests. Gradually, however, as Gierek's economic boom waned, the Party re-imposed its traditional controls. Union activists like Walesa were expected to obey orders, to act as a "transmission belt" between the

how to administer it. This explains why I can control crowds and strikes so well. One has to be very angry in order to know how to control the anger of the people. One has to have learned how to live with it in oneself." A final lesson that Walesa drew from December 1970 was not to trust the promises of politicians. The replacement that month of the increasingly authoritarian Wladyslaw Gomulka by Edward Gierek fueled hopes for change. Many Poles believed in Gierek, as they had believed in Gomulka before him. When he appealed to them with his slogan "Will you help me?", they responded. A bluff ex-miner from the industrial region of Silesia, he seemed like a breath of fresh air after the austere Gomulka. Walesa met Gierek for the first and only time on 25 January 1971. Poland's new leader was making a personal tour of the Baltic ports in an attempt to repair ties between the Communist party and the workers. In Gdansk, as in Szczecin, he held lengthy talks with worker representatives, among them Walesa. In the light of subsequent events, the transcripts of these encounters make depressing reading. The excuses and promises made by Gierek

Communist party and workers.

The crunch for Walesa personally came in March 1976. Accused of "disorderly conduct" during a trade union meeting, he was sacked from the shipyard. In fact, he had been protesting against poor working conditions and preparing a list of grievances to submit to the management. Disgusted by what he regarded as the double-talk

Danuta Walesa (below) *in the kitchen of the two-room apartment in Gdansk, and* (right) *with Bogdan, Slawomir, Przemyslaw, and Jaroslaw. During the four years from 1976 she saw little of her husband, whose time was taken up with the fight for free unions. While he was in and out of prison, and going from one meeting to another, it was left to her to act as the stable center of the family.*

of the union's leaders, he remarked at the meeting—a little too loudly—"I'm staying home from now on."
Later that year, Walesa made contact with the dissident "Workers' Defense Committee" (KOR) formed to protect workers harassed and imprisoned by the authorities following new riots over increases in the price of food. Thus began Walesa's underground struggle for free trade unions. Over the next four years, he was detained several hundred times by police for periods of up to 48 hours. (Above this limit, formal charges have to be made.)
Danuta Walesa complained that she rarely saw her husband during this period. His life was an endless round of secret meetings, prison, and propagating the cause. Danuta was left to bring up their children in their tiny tworoom apartment in a drab Gdansk suburb. When their sixth child, Anna, was born, Lech was in jail and unable to visit his wife. Later he paid tribute to Danuta's patience, saying that any other woman would have stuck a carving knife through him long before.

Walesa, however, made good use of his spells in prison. Like many other revolutionary leaders, he looked on jail as a time to gain much-needed rest and to think through what he wanted to do with his life. On being released, he would take every opportunity of telling as many people as possible about his experiences. This made him a fairly well-known figure in Gdansk. A Western visitor who met Walesa in Gdansk in early 1980 recalled that, during a taxi ride, he spent the entire time trying to convert the driver to the idea of independent unions.
Unofficial union cells began making their appearance in Poland in late 1977. The first was one in Radom, scene of clashes between workers and police the previous year. On 29 April 1978, dissidents in Gdansk—Walesa among them—announced the formation of a "Baltic Committee of the Free Independent Trade Union." Its aim was to defend "the economic, legal, and human rights" of all employees. At this stage, there were fewer than 100 active free trade unionists throughout the country. Because of

Walesa was arrested and imprisoned several hundred times on various charges connected with his union activities between 1976 and 1980.
One of these occasions coincided with the arrival of the youngest Walesa, Anna (below) with her mother. In prison when she was born, Walesa was unable to visit his wife and daughter.

police harassment, their influence on the shopfloor was very limited. But thanks to KOR, the movement did have its own four-page illegally printed fortnightly, *Robotnik* (The Worker).

In September 1979, *Robotnik* published a 1000-word charter of workers' rights. Among the signatories were Walesa, Anna Walentynowicz, Andrzej Gwiazda, and several other present-day Solidarity leaders. They described their primary long-term aim as "the establishment of independent trade unions," and called on other workers to "shake off the feeling of apathy, to stop passively accepting restrictions on our rights, the deterioration in our living conditions." The six-point list of demands included the indexing of wages to inflation, a 40-hour working week, improved work safety, abolition of privileges for party members, and guarantee of the right to strike. All these demands were to surface during the strikes that swept Poland a year later.

Outlining a plan of action, the signatories described strikes as a very effective weapon but added that their success was generally only short-term. They therefore advised: "In order not to waste the gains won in a strike, workers should elect representatives who can monitor the implementation of their demands. If employees act in solidarity, they can force the management to make concessions by the mere threat of strike."

The charter called for the formation of unofficial worker groups. Initially they could operate in secret: later they would reveal themselves in the form of independent workers' committees. It concluded: "Only independent trade unions, with the backing of the workers they represent, have a chance of challenging the authorities. Only they can represent a power with which the authorities will

A wall cannot be demolished with
butts of the head. We must move
slowly, step by step, otherwise the wall
remains untouched and we break our heads.

Lech Walesa

be obliged to negotiate on an equal footing." Until now, the Gdansk group did not have a leader. If anyone, it was Mrs. Walentynowicz rather than Walesa who acted as their spokesman. A Western journalist who met the whole group just before the shipyard strike recalled that Mrs. Walentynowicz did most of the talking while Walesa nodded in agreement. The group's main aim, she

The strain involved in organizing and leading Eastern Europe's first independent union is reflected in the face of its leader. Within six months the dissident electrician had become a figure of national importance.

explained, was to raise the workers' consciousness and teach them how to press their demands through the official trade unions. For his part, Walesa insisted on the need to operate openly to prove to the workers that there was no reason to fear the authorities.

Open activism was considered Walesa's special talent. He distributed *Robotnik* and other dissident publications out-

side factories, in trains and buses, or at church. He had a unique ability to whip up crowds which he regarded as automatic protection against the police.

One of the vehicles used by Walesa to spread his ideas was the anniversary of the December 1970 events. The anniversary was marked for the first time in 1978 when Walesa and Gwiazda managed to gather several hundred people outside Gate Number 2 of the Lenin shipyard, scene of the first killings of workers by police. The following year they did even better. A crowd of about 5,000 people turned up. A wreath was laid in honor of the dead and Walesa spoke on the subject of free unions. He also vowed that, the follwoing year, a monument would be erected to commemorate the dead shipyard workers—even if they all had to bring stones to build it themselves. This too later became a basic demand of the Gdansk strikers.

In the meantime, Walesa was losing one job after another. After his dismissal from the shipyard, he started working for a building company called Zrem. But he was laid off in January 1979 because of overdiligent union activity. Elected once again as a delegate to a conference of the official unions, he had protested against attempts from above to manipulate elections to the posts of president and secretary. "I asked them what this meant, what I was doing there at all—to take part in an election or just to applaud...that's how I found myself once again outside the factory gate," he recalled.

His next job was with an engineering firm, Electromontaz. His colleagues found him "friendly and reliable...an excellent workman." The management too was pleased; he was officially declared the company's outstanding electrician. The official attitude changed, however, after the demonstration he organized outside the shipyard in December 1979. Several weeks later, he was fired, this time for taking a day off without permission.

The Elektromontaz affair created quite a stir in Gdansk. Sacked along with Walesa were some 25 other workers, most of whom had taken part in the unauthorized ceremony. A "workers' commission" was formed with the

Important allies in Walesa's struggle for free unions were the members of KOR, the "Workers' Defense Committee" founded by Adam Michnik (left) and Jacek Kuron (right).

Below, volunteers working on the monument to those killed in 1970 fulfill Walesa's promise that a monument would be built even if the workers had to bring the stones themselves to do it.

open support of almost half the 500-strong workforce. The commission called brief strikes to demand the reinstatement of those dismissed, talks with the management over working conditions, and quarterly cost-of-living wage increases. Little came of the protests, but they did provide a foretaste of the trouble to come.

With hindsight, one can say the stage was now set for "the Polish August." Throughout the country, there was massive popular discontent at degrading living conditions, political repression, and increasing shortages of basic consumer goods. Confidence in the country's official institutions, and especially in Gierek himself, was virtually nil.

The dissidents, it is true, were few in number—but they were increasingly well organized. They also had a program for political change which centered on the establishment of independent unions. What is remarkable is that, despite all this, the force of the eruption still surprised men like Walesa. Certainly he expected increasing popular unrest, indeed he actively prepared for it. But he thought that progress toward free unions would only come gradually, not all of a sudden. In January, he confided in a visitor: "I'm sure we'll get free trade unions

in this country one day—but I doubt if it will be in my lifetime." Even after the strike had succeeded, and he was installed in the union's new offices, he told me that he had thought the government would be able to contain the crisis until at least 1981.

The fact that the explosion came much earlier was partly due to the ineptitude and mistakes of the Communist authorities themselves. At each stage of the crisis, they pursued a policy guaranteed to unite eighty percent of the Polish nation against them. By taking a tough position and attempting to divide different groups of workers, they succeeded only in antagonizing them. Then, when popular pressure became overwhelming, they retreated ignominiously. Instead of defusing the discontent through reforms, the government wasted all its energy fighting battles it could not win.

On the workers' side, Walesa and other strike leaders showed immense tactical sense. It was clear that they had learned from the mistakes of December 1970. What is more, Walesa in particular understood that the struggle was taking place at several different levels, and he changed his approach, even his tone of voice, to suit each particular audience.

A Polish journalist who watched Walesa closely throughout the eighteen-day occupation of the shipyard commented admiringly: "He acted like a true statesman. There were three important groups with whom he had to deal—the government negotiators, the delegates on the integrated strike committee, and the mass of ordinary people outside the gates. The outside gate crowd was not interested in the details of everything. They wanted a symbol for their hopes—and he behaved as a symbol. The delegates wanted a symbol too, but they also needed information and concrete instructions: Walesa provided it. As for Jagielski, the deputy prime minister, once the government was ready to talk, he wanted to do business— and with him Walesa was calm and businesslike." This explains the contrast in Walesa's character; his coolness and pragmatism while negotiating, his demagogic stance outside. But he knew how to keep the crowds under con-

The beginning of the end for Edward Gierek? A symbolic photo (never before published) shows a placard reading "Comrade Gierek, we're with you" left behind in an empty Warsaw stadium after a mass meeting for Party members in 1976.

Among his clandestine activities Walesa included selling copies of "Robotnik" (below), the illegally printed fortnightly of the "Baltic Committee of the Free Independent Trade Union," produced with the assistance of KOR.

trol, and appealed to them with his larger-than-life gestures and infectious good humor. His moustache of course made him easily identifiable. Other elements in his image included a lapel badge bearing the image of the Madonna of Czestochowa, Poland's patron saint, the wide grin, the huge pen emblazoned with the Pope's portrait with which he signed the Gdansk agreement, his constant—if tuneless—singing of the national anthem. He reflected the popular mood: allowing himself to be thrown high into the air, thrusting his clenched fists upward with joy, laughing with the people and expressing their anger in pithy, simple sentences.

At times of tension, he raised people's spirits by cracking jokes. I remember on the second day of the strike, when the outcome was still very uncertain, he had 5,000 shipyard workers in fits of laughter by making fun of his own predicament. "My wife will be furious when she finds out what I've done," he told the crowd. "I already have six children, so I guess the only way I can make it up to her is by giving her a seventh." Later, he complained that his ten-year-old son was causing him problems. "He went to school the other day and threatened his headmaster with a strike unless the teachers behaved themselves."

Much of Walesa's style was based on a conscious rejection of officialdom. He behaved as the antithesis of a Communist party apparatchik. In part, the strikes were a reaction against what many Poles regarded as a mendacious world, a foreign way of thinking imposed upon them from outside. Walesa shunned convoluted ideological expressions. He delighted in telling the crowds: "I am not your master, I am your servant." As a Polish official remarked: "That was a direct slap in the face to the whole style of political leadership to which Poland has been subjected for the last thirty-five years."

Perhaps one of his greatest assets as the leader of Solidarity is Walesa's absolute identification with the members of his union. His own background is the same as theirs, and he shares their aspirations. Seen here outside the door of their apartment block in Gdansk, and (right) inside their two-room apartment in November 1980, the Walesas do appear very much as the personification of the average Polish working family.

workers' state, after all, what could be more natural than that the proletariat should want to exercise its theoretical power? There is nothing in Marx and Lenin which says that Party members should be a privileged class or that the police should be above the law. As a slogan slung up across the gates of the Lenin shipyard expressed it: "Workers of all factories, unite!"

If pressed, Walesa would probably favor a rudimentary "brotherhood of man" type socialism based on the principles of equality and human dignity. But his strength is that he does not think in ideological terms. During the strike, he was asked whether free trade unions were compatible with communism. His reply was that of the practical worker rather than the ideologue: "Call it what you will, but it has to be efficient...if something gets jammed and breaks down, then either we throw it away or we do something else. Since I have had the experience of 1956, 1968, 1970, 1976, and now 1980, I know that these breakdowns are ever more frequent in Poland. There is little point in carrying out repairs. We might as well buy a new machine."

At the same time, Walesa's outlook was shaped by the fact that he had been brought up under a socialist system. He rejects Marxist dogma—but he has never expressed any particular fondness for capitalism. Given Poland's conditions, he regards independent unions as a better guarantee of democracy than competing political parties in a Western-style parliament. His attitude to politics was expressed in the comment "We don't want to go back to capitalism or copy Western models. We live in Poland and we must find Polish solutions. Socialism isn't a bad system. Let it remain—as long as it's controlled." On another occasion, he said workers couldn't possibly be in favor of the factories' reverting to capitalist ownership. "In our country, things are simpler than they are in the West since we all form the state and we are closer to responsibility...it's not a question of being communist or socialist or capitalist. What matters is that each system should be human. It should be for the people and with the people."

Walesa sometimes adopted a deliberately ingenuous approach to ideological questions, taking the regime's own slogans at their face value. If People's Poland was a

Throughout the protracted negotiations in Gdansk, Walesa insisted on speaking the simple Polish that everybody could understand. In hindsight, this battle for the purity of the language was just as important as the battle for the twenty-one demands ranging from independent unions to freer access to the mass media. It provided a foretaste of what was later to become the driving force of the Solidarity movement: the idea that Poland should regain its national heritage—or, in Walesa's words, that "Poland should become Poland again."

At the start of the talks, Walesa asked the government delegation to take a stand on the workers' demands. The government representative replied: "Allow me to answer in a general way." Walesa: "No, we want a concrete answer. Point by point."

It was a crucial victory. For years, Poland had been living in a kind of "Alice in Wonderland" world where words and phrases had lost their meaning—and had been twisted to suit passing political needs. Part of Poland's August revolution lay in stripping away the fantasy and revealing the hollowness that lay beneath the bombastic slogans of the Gierek years. The workers, Walesa among them, distrusted generalized language and theoretical expressions.

One of the shipyard delegates summed up the workers' attitude: "Better the bitter truth than a sweet lie. Sweets are for children, we are grown-ups."

A related issue was that of dignified behavior. Walesa insisted that the shipyard workers conduct themselves in an honorable manner. Drink was banned right from the start—and this became a matter of considerable pride with the strikers. Discipline was strict: the biggest punishment of all was to be excluded from the strike. Once, when a worker disgraced the strikers, Walesa insisted that he be treated correctly. Grabbing a microphone, he said: "I appeal to everyone to allow this man to leave the shipyard peacefully and without insults. I ask for dignified and noble behavior."

Walesa's quality was that he managed to balance within himself the two main strands in the Polish character: romanticism and realism. Reflecting on the strike after-

The Pen with the Pope (left). *To sign the Gdansk agreement Walesa used a giant ballpoint pen bearing a picture of the Pope, which subsequently became a part of his persona, along with his spontaneous gestures of enthusiasm* (right). *Both reflected an instinctive ability to communicate both verbally and nonverbally with his fellow workers.*

wards, one of his chief advisers, Bronislaw Geremek, told me, "If it had not been for the romantic element in our national traditions, then we could not have won the victory of last August. The workers believed that they could achieve what the rest of the world thought was impossible. But, in order to see this victory through, it was also necessary to think realistically—to know when to compromise."

Walesa understood the art of compromise. He knew when to stop and consolidate his gains. A vital moment came right at the end of the Gdansk general strike when a militant group of workers opposed a clause in the agreement stipulating that the new independent unions would accept "the leading role of the Communist party." Walesa argued with them, warning that if they pushed for too much, they risked losing everything. This too was later to become a recurring theme in fights within Solidarity.

Victory, when it came, tasted sweet. Standing side by side with the deputy prime minister, Jagielski, Walesa made a statement that turned him into a national figure. The signing ceremony on 31 August was televised throughout Poland, providing the vast majority of Poles with their first glimpse of Walesa. He projected his image by signing the agreement with a huge ballpoint pen topped by a portrait of Pope John Paul II. As usual, he addressed his audience off the cuff:

"Our dispute has been brought to an end without resorting to force, by means of talks and arguments. We have proved that Poles, if they wish to do so, can always come to an understanding. I always speak frankly and say what I think. I speak frankly now too. We haven't achieved everything, but we have achieved everything possible under the circumstances. We will also achieve the rest, since we now have the most important thing: our independent, self-governing trade union. This is our guarantee for the future.

"We have fought not only for ourselves and for our own interests but also for the country as a whole. You know, all of you, what great solidarity the working people, the entire country has shown with our struggle."

The Solidarity movement was born.

The next day, 1 September, the anniversary of Hitler's attack on Poland, Walesa moved into his new makeshift headquarters, a rambling apartment in a Gdansk suburb. Neighbors looked on in amazement as Poland's newfound hero announced to crowds of reporters by the front door: "I am not interested in politics. I am a union man. My job now is to organize the union."

Walesa immediately found himself the focus of popular hopes. Millions of Poles looked to him for leadership. Messages poured into Gdansk seeking instructions. It was a novel situation for an unemployed electrician and unsung dissident. Suddenly, almost overnight, he found himself at the head of a major—and rapidly growing—organization. Inevitably, the transition from being the voice of revolutionary discontent to the manager of a bureaucratic apparatus was not an easy one to make.

I visited Walesa soon after he moved into his new office. The scene was chaotic—dozens of people milling around waiting for something to happen—but the outline of an organization was already visible. Walesa was accompanied everywhere by a bodyguard, a tough shipyard worker who clung to him like a sheepdog. Interviews with the press were rationed to five minutes and, at the end, Walesa would jump up and leave like the chief cowboy in a western—taking half the room with him. It was as though he was still psyched up with nervous energy, but so busy that he had little time to reflect where either he or the union was going.

He was learning to cope with fame. When he appeared at a Solidarity meeting, the crowds chanted his nickname: "Leszek! Leszek!" When he walked down a street, people pressed forward to ask for his autograph or shake his hand. At his parish church, prayers were said for his soul "so that he may lead us to freedom." Letters and messages of support poured in constantly. One, typical, family wrote to express "our gratitude and respect for your wis-

The old kitchen (p. 102) has given way to something rather better, in a new six-room apartment in Gdansk (below), though among the penalties of Walesa's new role as a symbol could be included photographers in the bathroom (right). The union leader's star status and the reception he was everywhere accorded (far right, outside the Tribunal in Warsaw, during the registration of Solidarity) aroused resentment, however, when it spilled over into union affairs.

dom and bravery in leading the struggle for human rights."

Walesa seemed to enjoy being a symbol, even though he found it irritating and exhausting at the same time. His way of life had changed for good. His family moved out of the cramped two-room flat into a six-room apartment in a modern Gdansk suburb provided by the Mayor of Gdansk. But Walesa was hardly ever alone with them. During the rare moments he spent at home, as likely as not a journalist or film crew would show up to interview his children or photograph him in the shower. There were so many visitors that his wife described the house as "a windmill."

Walesa felt trapped by all the publicity. A man of simple tastes and pleasures, he suddenly found that he had to live up to a new exalted image. He complained it was impossible for him to talk to a pretty girl or drink a beer without someone censoring his behavior. When he was seen in the nightclub of the Victoria-Intercontinental Hotel in Warsaw, the incident triggered off a storm of criticism from his more puritan followers.

Many of Solidarity's leaders are ascetics willing to subordinate everything to the cause. Walesa is not. He liked to be able to escape and be himself.

Inevitably, success changed him—although he said it didn't. Outwardly, he put on weight and his once lean face gathered extra flesh. His wardrobe multiplied from one suit to half a dozen and friends kept him supplied with a steady stream of imported cigarettes. "Why is it that I can't smoke Western cigarettes like everyone else?" he joked when he was accused of adopting bourgeoise tastes. Later, on his doctor's advice, he dropped smoking them and started puffing sagely at a pipe.

He used to say he couldn't care a fig for generals, journa-

lists, priests, and politicans. That too was all part of the image. In fact he did pay great attention to other people's opinions, so much so that he was frequently accused of over-flexibility. At the same time, he was also capable of shutting his ears and doggedly following his own instincts.

His new-found star status annoyed some people in Solidarity. I remember when Walesa first came to Warsaw in September to lodge Solidarity's statutes with a district court. He arrived in a tourist bus with some 50 other union delegates—and was hailed as a savior by hundreds of supporters gathered on the steps of the courthouse. After appearing in court, he led an impromptu march through the city, gathering followers as he went like a Polish Pied Piper. Back in the bus, a disgruntled delegate sat by himself. Waving bitterly in Walesa's direction, he remarked: "I came here to register a union—not to take

part in a circus." And other voices were to be heard criticizing him for arrogance. In an early television interview, he took a flippant approach toward a journalist, which disappointed many people. No doubt he was trying to put the interviewer, a stooge of officialdom, in his place. But many viewers regarded Walesa's style as a snub to their own intelligence. They didn't like his behavior. It angered them when their hero did not live up to their expectations.

Walesa showed little enthusiasm for the details of running a union. At meetings of Solidarity's national presidium, he frequently displayed his impatience. He would pull funny faces for the photographers who followed him round, shake his head in annoyance, or sometimes even doze off as one seemingly interminable speech succeeded another. Then he would suddenly wake up and try to railroad his own ideas through the meeting.

In general, Walesa has seemed to enjoy, and cope with, his new status as a media star. It was indeed his proposal that the events in Gdansk should be fully reported, which entailed free access for journalists, and he has remained constant to this principle, presumably recognizing not only the need to ensure that all Poles know exactly what is going on in Solidarity, but also his own considerable value as a symbol, both at home and abroad, of the process of renewal.

That there must, though, have been times when it felt as if the process of renewal was getting out of control, is reflected in the picturees on these pages.
Below: *Journalists and cameramen in the Walesas' apartment.* Right: *An extraordinary scene during Mass at the Lenin shipyard, on the last day of the strike.*

By contrast, he is at his best when handling ordinary workers. He is a tremendously skillful speaker, knowing how to give vent to popular grievances but at the same time persuade the crowd to follow his lead. One trick he employed frequently when trying to defuse a strike was to use militant rhetoric to disguise an essentially moderate position. He tried to contain the people's anger by getting them to laugh at corrupt Communist party officials rather than inciting them to action.

When demands for retribution were raised, he would invariably reply: "We'll get round to that eventually, but in the meantime there aren't enough prisons in Poland to hold all the officials who should be locked up. And, after all, why should we feed them at our expense?"

Soon after the union was formed, Walesa faced a split among his advisers. They were divided into two groups: the Catholic intellectuals who had helped him draft the Gdansk agreement, and the dissidents around KOR who

Walesa's first trip abroad was as part of a Solidarity delegation to visit Italian unions, and of course his compatriot the Pope. Below: In the airplane en route for Italy are the Walesas, Anna Walentinowicz, and Tadeusz Mazowiecki. The highlight of the visit was perhaps the meeting between today's two best known Poles (right), but there was also time amid the official functions for sightseeing and shopping. Below, a picture that would go straight to the heart of any Polish housewife. Together with her father-in-law Stanislas (far right) who came over from America for the visit, Mrs. Walesa inspects the rich array of sausages at a delicatessen.

decades. Like many other Poles, Walesa saw Wyszynski as the protector of national traditions and esteemed him even more highly than the Polish-born Pontiff, Pope John Paul II.

Some months later, Walesa started complaining in public about his advisers. He made fun of the intellectuals, saying they were so clever that it took them hours to reach a decision on a problem he could resolve in five minutes. As for the dissidents, he paid tribute to KOR for laying the foundation stone to Solidarity. "But now," he said, "we have outgrown our teachers. They should go along with us and not try to foist alien elements onto us. Why should we be held responsible for their actions?"

had provided the basis for the free trade union movement in Poland. Walesa felt an obligation to both groups and, initially, seemed torn between the different sets of advice he was receiving. By and large, the intellectuals tended to be more cautious, preferring to consolidate gains already made, while the dissidents believed it was impossible to prevent the escalation of new demands.

Eventually, the differences between the two groups were smoothed over. Largely due to the governement's own intransigence, rank and file sentiment within the union became increasingly militant. The Catholics realized that, if Solidarity's survival was at stake, the movement could not simply restrict itself to trade union activities. The dissidents, meanwhile, understood it was necessaery to calm down popular passions. Jacek Kuron and other KOR leaders helped call off several strikes. As for Walesa, he tried to turn the diversity of opinions within Solidarity into a source of strength. "We have had enough unanimity in this country," he said.

Walesa described the late Primate of Poland, Cardinal Stefan Wyszynski, as "my number one adviser." He openly revered the 79-year-old cardinal who had provided the spiritual inspiration for Solidarity by stubbornly defending the Church's independence for over three

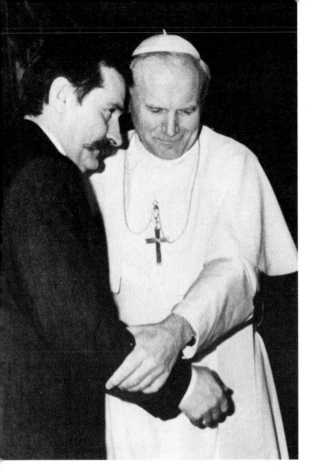

Cardinal Wyszynski, however, he never criticized.

Another indication of Walesa's loyalities was provided by the large crucifix that hung on his wall at the Morski Hotel in Gdansk which became Solidarity's home in mid-September. Solidarity, he said, was not founded as a Christian organization. But, "As long as I am chairman of the union, the crucifix will hang here." It was a gesture that drew some complaints from atheist members of the union—as was the decision to include a large number of priests in the delegation that visited Rome in January 1981. But Walesa's Catholicism reflected the feelings of the rank and file.

After an unsteady start, Walesa enjoyed good relations with leading Communist officials. Initially he had to reject several offers from the government, including the suggestion that he become head of the official trade unions. Later the regime understood that Walesa was more valuable to them uncorrupted, as a popular leader trusted by the people, who could be relied upon to urge the cause of moderation. The political outcast was accepted as an equal negotiating partner by the Communist state.

Walesa's great strength as Solidarity's leader was that he was so obviously a worker himself. As one commentator remarked: "A more working-class worker the working class never produced." The government was forced to accept him as a representative of the workers. The workers regarded him as one of their own.

As during the August strike, so too during the subsequent confrontations with the government, Walesa placed great store on unity. It was the source of the union's power, but also its principal weakness. On several occasions, moderate leaders like Walesa found themselves forced to keep pace with the militants...just to preserve union solidarity.

A good example of this occurred in February 1981 when Solidarity members in the southern towns of Bielsko-Biala and Jelena Gora started protests over local issues involving corruption and mismanagement. Convinced that their cause was just, they were determined to fight to the bitter end. Unlike Walesa, they did not see the dispute in a national political context, as a possibly dangerous move in the increasingly intricate war of nerves being waged between the Kremlin, the Polish leadership, and Solidarity. For the local activists, it was simply a question of right and wrong.

After a general strike had been going on in Bielsko-Biala for some days, Walesa decided that the protest would

Walesa professes considerable admiration for the Japanese economy, and Solidarity was not slow to return the visit of Japanese union leaders to Poland in 1980. Right: Walesa arrives in Japan, in May 1981. Below: The crowd of photographers awaiting his arrival at a factory in Osaka. Bottom right: Relaxing in Japanese style at Kyoto.

安全＋第一
SAFETY ✚ FIRST

have to be defused. He rushed to the town from Warsaw like a one-man fire brigade in a white Mercedes bus. But, once there, he found that his only way of influencing the strikers was to lead them.

I attended a press conference given by Walesa in Bielsko-Biala. It was like en elaborate game. Smiling and puffing his pipe, he told us that several hundred thousand people were listening in through an ingenious telephone hookup system. He fully supported the strikers' demands for the dimissal of half a dozen corrupt officials: the strike would only end, he said, if the guilty were removed.

And that was indeed what happened...the next day. It was a victory for the strikers, but a very risky one. Walesa questioned their choice of tactics and understood the consequences of unrestrained confrontation with the government. But he also knew that unless the union stuck together all would be lost.

An even more serious trial of strength came with the Byd-

The assassination attempt on John Paul II occurred during Walesa's visit to Japan. Here, at breakfast, he is able to read in the newspaper that the Pope's recovery is making progress.
Below: *Against a backdrop of Solidarity in Polish and Japanese, and a model of the Gdansk memorial, Walesa addresses a meeting of Japanese trade unionists.*

goszcz affair in March when Solidarity activists were beaten up by police. But this time Walesa managed to play the Solidarity card to his own advantage. At a meeting of the union's national committee, he threatened to resign if the union proclaimed an immediate general strike throughout Poland. Instead he favored a four-hour "warning" strike, allowing time for negotiations to take place with the authorities. After an emotional scene, his

plan was finally adopted. Walesa outlined his political philosophy during a long meeting with Warsaw steelworkers at the height of the crisis. He told them they should take every precaution possible to avoid taking the regime head on. The other side must be given a chance to get off the hook, otherwise everything might end in bloodshed. Solidarity should be patient and prepared to compromise on some of its demands. At the same time,

Walesa also made clear that Solidarity would not give way on essential issues.

There was no point exchanging one corrupt politician for another. What was important, however, was to gradually change the system so that all public officials gradually became subject to social control.

The Bydgoszcz episode proved a cathartic experience both for Walesa and for Poland. Walesa's moderate line eventually prevailed, but the crisis exposed a lot of raw nerves in the union. The decision to call off the threatened general strike was endorsed by a majority of members—but many objected to the way Walesa had taken it virtually alone without consulting anybody else. Walesa's argument was that the situation was so tense and dangerous that he had to take responsibility upon himself, rather than entrust it to the cranky machinery of democracy. If the right decision was taken, who worried about the mechanics?

In fact a lot of people did care. Democracy had been trampled upon for so many years in Poland that it had become a particularly sensitive issue. Criticism of Walesa's autocratic methods flared up at a meeting of Solidarity's national committee soon afterwards. The attack was led by the union's press spokesman, Karol Modzelewski, who accused Walesa of behaving like a king surrounded by a subservient court.

At issue was the union's decision-making process which Modzelewski described as "monarchic." Referring to Walesa, he said: "We have enthroned a king—and arround him there is a court and a parliament. But, since the king refuses to be just a decorative figure, it is the court that rules—and not the parliament. This is an enor-

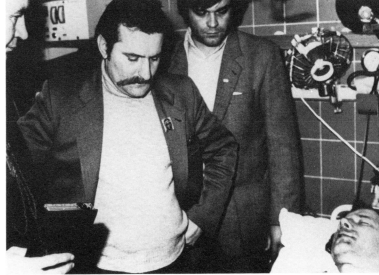

Jan Rulewski, in hospital after being beaten up at Bydgoszcz, is visited by Walesa (below). One of the most severe critics of Walesa's moderate approach, he is nonetheless aware of the importance for Solidarity of Walesa as the clearly identifiable leader of the union.

mous threat to the union. It could lead to a situation where every criticism is regarded as a conspiracy and an attack on Walesa is construed as an attempt to grab power in the union. This mechanism, which has been borrowed from a totalitarian system, could turn the union into a copy of the Communist party."

Modzelewski, whose personal relations with Walesa had long been bad, resigned as press spokesman following his attack. Similar, if less harshly worded, criticism came from Gwiazda—Solidarity's deputy chairman—in an open letter to Walesa. He too warned of the danger of autocratic leadership, of allowing the experts too much influence. Solidarity, he wrote, must remember the values for which it fought. The principle of democracy had been broken—and could be restored only by complete openness and the full flow of information.

Walesa was unrepentant. He believed in democracy as much as anybody, but he also felt a responsibility for Poland. He told Solidarity's national committee: "We must proceed cautiously. We must be courageous, but also reasonable. The world admires us for walking a tightrope without falling off. It asks us to keep our balance,

and we must take this into account." In frequent newspaper interviews, he was to elaborate on his theme. "Some of our activists have proved themselves during times of struggle and conflict, but have failed to adapt themselves to new conditions. These constant struggles exhaust us both mentally and physically. The queues outside the shops become longer and so therefore we only harm ourselves. We must look for other ways than strikes to settle our grievances....We live on the edge of a precipice so we must not take risks. Much can be attained gradually step by step.

Sometimes he expressed the wish to retire, saying he was dead tired and in poor health. After all his triumphs, he told Oriana Fallaci that from now on he could only descend. "If the worst happens, all the rage of the people will turn on me. The same ones who applauded me, erected altars for me, will trample on me. They will even forget that I acted in good faith. If I were selfish and shrewd, I would cut my moustache and go back to some shipyard. But I cannot do it. The situation will become more and more complicated and we are going to receive many blows...but I must stay where I am to struggle, to

A meditative Lech Walesa walking in the Polish countryside. After the strain of the past year he talks of retirement and his desire for a quieter life. In the meantime, however, there is Solidarity....

extinguish the unnecessary fires, to transform the movement into an organization.''

An interesting comment about Walesa was made to me by one of his severest critics, Jan Rulewski, the Solidarity leader in Bydgoszcz. He was among the activists beaten up by police and he later accused Walesa of compromising over "the workers' blood." But he also acknowledged that Walesa was indispensible to Solidarity. "Poland has a psychological need for a leader who will allow us to go to bed peacefully in the knowledge that there's someone we trust who stands guard over us. For half a century, we have had no such man. But now we have Walesa and, whatever else we do, we have to stick with him."

Only history can really assess Lech Walesa. The Polish drama has not yet been fully played out. But looking back at the revolution of which he is a symbol, I think that what happened was inevitable. The fact that the Lenin shipyard went on strike on Thursday 14 August may have been very largely due to Walesa. The fact that the shipyard workers continued their strike in solidarity with other workers in Gdansk, even after their own demands had been settled, may also have been due to him. But, with or without Walesa, I believe that much the same kind of process would have taken place. Polish history was moving inexorably in that direction.

This is not to belittle Walesa's achievement. He is great not because he changed the course of history, but because he was the symbol chosen by history to voice the grievances of the Polish nation. His character perfectly matched the needs of the moment. By August 1980, revolutionary discontent had reached such a pitch that the dam had to burst somewhere. Walesa's experience and wisdom proved decisive in steering the unrest in an orderly direction. But, if Walesa had not appeared, the chances are that history would have thrown up someone else with equally bitter memories and hard-won experience.

The truth is that Poland was waiting for its Lech Walesa.

PICTURE CREDITS

INDEX

Numbers in italics refer to illustrations

BBC, Hulton Picture Library, London: 16 left

CAF, Warsaw: 21 below

Keystone Press, Zurich: 42, 43

Niedenthal, Chris, Warsaw: 2 above, 8 top, 10/11, 23 below, 30, 35, 36 left, 38, 46, 47, 54, 55, 56 above left and above right, 58/59, 60, 62 above right, 65, 66/67, 67, 68 top, 69 top, 70 top, 71 top left and top center, 72 top and bottom, 73 top left and top center, 75 bottom, 76 top and center, 78, 79, 81, 84 center, 85, 88 right, 94 top, 95 center right and bottom, 96, 96/97, 97, 105, 106 top right, 107 left, 108, 108/109, 110 center, 117, 123 top and bottom

Ringier Bilderdienst, Zurich: 26 below, 27, 28, 29

Sipa-Press, Paris: 26 center left and center right, 40, 45 below left and below right, 53 right, 110 bottom, 113, 123 right
Boccon Gibod: 72 left, 73 center right and bottom
Goess: 31, 32, 33, 41
Laski: 2 below, 3, 6/7, 7, 8 center and bottom, 9, 12, 13, 16/17, 18 above left and below left, 20/21, 22 left, 34, 37 right, 39 left, 44, 45 above left and above right, 50/51, 52 left, 56 below, 57, 62 above left, below, 62/63, 63, 64, 66, 68 left and bottom, 69 center, 70 below, 71 top right, 74 top right and bottom, 75 top left and top right, 76 bottom, 77, 80 left and center, 82, 82/83, 84 top, 89 right, 91 right, 92/93, 94 bottom, 95 top and center left, 98, 99, 100, 101, 102, 103, 104, 106 top left and center left, 107 right, 111, 112, 114, 115, 116, 118, 119, 120, 121, 122, 125
Loor: 61, 74 top left, 80 right, 89 left, 94 center, 110 top
Nadal: 5, 39 right, 48, 49, 52/53, 86/87, 88 left, 90, 91 left
Setboum: 36/37

The Fort Ticonderoga Museum: 14 left

Ullstein Bilderdienst, Berlin: 18/19, 19, 20 below, 22 right, 23 above and right, 24, 24/25

Afghanistan, 57, 85
America 98, 118
American Revolution 14
Anders, General Wladislaw, 20
Andrzejewski, Jerzi, 33, 42
Anti-nazi Resistance, 20
Anti-Semitism, 78, 79
Appeal of the Sixty Four, 68
Armia Kraieva (AK), 20, 22, 23, 24, 33
Armia Ludewa (AL), 22, 33
Augustus II, 14
Auschwitz, 23
Austria-Hungary, 13, 15
Autocratic government, 35

Babiuch, Edward, 60
Baltic Committee of the Free Independent Trade Union, 102, 107
Baltic Corridor, 18
Baltic Free Trade Union, 88
Barcikowski, Kazimierz, 60
Beck, Josef, 19
Belgium, 38
Belorussia, 18
Bielsko-Biala, 73, 119, 120
Bierut, Boleslaw, 27, 29
Blitzkrieg, 21
Boleslaw III, 13
Bolshevism, 16
Bolshevization of Poland, 23
Bratislava, 41
Brezhnev, Leonid, 57, 71, 77, 80, 84, 85
Brzezinski, Zbigniew, 84
Budapest, 40
Bujak, Zbigniew, 67, 69, 79
Bydgoszcz, 74–76, 77, 95, 121, 122, 123

Capitalism, 110
Carter, James E., 84
Casaroli, Monsignor, 46
Casimir III the Great, 13
Castle Square, 26, 31
Catholicism, 35, 39, 100
Ceausescu, Nicolae, 57
Cegielski factory, 28
Central Committee, 29, 30, 46, 60, 72, 75, 80
Charter of Workers' Rights, 103

Churchill, Winston S., 26
Collectivization, 27
Cominform, 27
Comintern, 20
Communist party, Polish, 9, 28, 43, 56, 60, 64, 70–73, 78–81
Confederation of Independant Poland, 70
Cracow, 36, 46, 94
Cyrankiewicz, Jozef, 38
Czechoslovakia, 19, 37, 65, 82, 85, 86

Danzig, *now* Gdansk, *q.v.*
Democratic Alliance, 30
Democratic Bloc, 24, 29
Democratic consultation, 41
Democratic party, 24
Dissidents, 70, 104, 106
Dubcek, Alexander, 41, 86
Duchy of Warsaw, 15

Eastern Front, 23
Eastern Pact, 19
East Germany, 74, 82
Elektromontaz, 104
England, 14
Europe, 10, 16, 23, 33
European Communist parties, 27
European Front, 20
Expansionism, 19

Finder, Pawel, 22
First Polish Army, 23
Fiszbach, Tadeusz, 54, 60
France, 19, 38, 68, 81
French Communist party, 38
French Revolution, 15

Gandhi, Mahatma, 86
Gdansk, 18, 20, 37 f., 44, 45, 52–72 passim, 62, 63, 72, 80–125 passim, 84, 96, 97
Gdansk Agreement, 66, 91, 113
Gdynia, 44, 53, 62
General strike, 65, 72, 75, 77, 121
Geneva, 7
Geremek, Bronislaw, 68, 113
Germanization, 15
Germany, 13, 14, 19–21, 42, 97, 98
Gestapo, 22

Gibraltar, 21
Gierek, Edward, 38, 39, 41, 46, 47, 53, 56, 57, 60, 64, 65, 73, 81, 101, 106, 107, 111
Gniech, Klemens, 54, 88–90
Gniezno, 13
Golendzinow, 60
Gomulka, Wladislaw, 22, 26, 27, 29, 34, 35, 38, 39, 43, 44, 46, 56, 57, 71, 101
Gorgow, 46
Government in Exile, Polish, 22, 23
Grand army, 15
Grunwald Patriotic Association, 79
Gwiazda, Andrzej, 53, 62, 64, 103, 104, 123

Hitler, Adolf, 19, 20, 21, 24, 113
Hoffman, General, 82
Holy Roman Empire, 13
Holy See, 13
Home Army (AK), see Armia Kraieva
Human rights, 72
Hungary, 30, 40, 65
Huta Warszawa, 8, 70, 75, 122

Ideological pluralism, 12
Imperialism, 7
Independence, 16
Industrialization, 27
Interfactory Strike Committee, see MKS
International Labor Organization, 7
Italy, 68, 119

Jablonna, 48
Japan, 120
Jagiellon dynasty, 13
Jagielski, Mieczyslaw, 52, 55, 60, 61, 64, 69, 106, 113
Jankowski, Romuald, 60
Jaroszewicz, Piotr, 41, 46
Jaruzelski, General Wojciech, 9, 57, 71, 74, 82, 84
Jasna Gora monastery, 43, 123
Jastrzebie, 45
Jaszczuk, 38
Jelena Gora, 119
Jews, 23
John Paul II, 36, 37, 46, 87, 110, 113, 118, 119, 121

Kania, Stanislaw, 9, 57, 60, 64, 65, 71–73, 78–80
Katowice, 38
Katyn massacre, 20, 22, 23
Khrushchev, Nikita S., 28–30
Kiev, 18
Kliszto, 29, 38
Kocilek, Stansilaw, 37
Koniew, Marshal, 30
KOR (Workers' Self-defense Committee), 37, 42, 49, 65, 68–71, 102, 103, 105, 107, 116, 118
Kosciecwicz, Judge, 74
Kosciuszko, Tadeusz, 14, 15
Kotodziej, Bogdan, 53
Koulikov, Marshal, 74
Kowalik, Tadeusz, 68
Kremlin, 57, 87, 119
KRP (National Coordination Committee), 67
Kuczynski, Wlademar, 68
Kulaj, Jan, 76
Kulikov, General, 82
Kuron, Jacek, 37, 42, 65, 69, 70, 71, 74, 79, 106, 118
Kyoto, 120

Labentowicz, Mariusz, 78
Lange, Professor, 34
Lenin, Vladimir I., 9, 86, 110
Lenin Shipyard, 48, 52, 53, 54, 57, 60, 62, 67, 70, 89, 91, 97, 99, 104, 110, 116, 125
Limited sovereignty, 57
Lipinski, Edward, 42, 68
Lis, Bogdan, 53, 64
Lithuania, 13, 18
Lodz, 67
Loga-Sowinski, Ignacy, 29, 38
London, 20, 23
Lublin, 37, 49, 52, 76
Luxemburg, Rosa, 15

Mach, Mieczyslaw, 74
Madonna of Czestechowa, 31, 100, 107, 123
Manchuria, 21
Marx, Karl, 110
Marxism, 12
Mazowiecki, Tadeusz, 68, 118

Michnik, Adam, 37, 42, 69, 70, 71, 79, 106
Middle East, 20
Mieszko, 13
Mikolajczyk, Stansilaw, 21, 24, 26
Mikolajska, Helena, 68
Mikoyan, Anastas, 29
MKS, 53, 55, 60, 66, 67
Mocyulski, Lesyek, 70
Modzelewski, Karol, 37, 67, 70, 122, 123
Mologec, Boleslaw, 22
Molotov, Wjatscheslaw, 20, 29
Mongols, 13
Monte Cassino, 23, 119
Moscow, 7, 8, 18, 21, 22, 57, 71, 75, 84, 85
Movement for Free Trade Unions, 52

Napoleon, 15
Norodniak, Jan, 75
National Council of Trade Unions (CRZZ), 60
National consciousness, 10, 13
National Guard, 22
National identity, 57
National unity, 23
National Security Council, 84
NATO, 87
Nazi Party, 20
Non-aggression pact, 19
Northern War, 14
Nowa Huta, 8, 75
Nowotko, 22

Ochab, Edward, 29
Oder/Neisse line, 26
Olstyn, 46
Olszowski, Stefan, 9, 71, 73, 75, 79
Opole Stare, 35
Osaka, 120
Otto I, 13
Otwock, 82

Paris, 85
Paul VI, 46
Pawlowski, 45
People's Army, see Armia Ludewa
Piast Kingdom, 13
Pilsudski, Marshal Jozef, 15, 16, 18, 19, 60

Pinkowska, Alicja, 69, 70
Piotrkow, 13
Pogrom, 79
Polityka, 57, 80
Polish Peasant party, 21, 24, 26
Polish Socialist party, 26
Polish-Soviet War, 18
Polish United Workers' party, 27, 30
Polish Workers' party, 22, 24, 26
Politburo, 9, 29, 30, 37, 60, 73
Pomerania, 13, 26
Poncet, Jean-François, 48
Poniatowsky, Prince Jozef, 14
Popov, 94
Potsdam, 24, 26
Powazki Cemetery, 22, 23, 47
Poznan, 28, 30, 42, 43
Pracobiorcy, 72
Pracodawcy, 72
Praga, 23
Prague Spring, 78, 86
Proletarian internationalism, 15
Prospotu, 33
Provisional Government of National Unity,
   24
Prussia, 13, 15, 26, 96
Pyka, Tadeusz, 53, 60

Radom, 41, 42, 56, 70, 74, 102
Rapacki, Adam, 78
Reagan, Ronald, 85
Red Army, 20, 23, 24
Red bourgeoisie, 80
Red Cross, 21, 24
Reunification of Poland, 16
Revolution, Russian, 16
Ribbentrop, Joachim von, 20
Robespierre, Maximilien de, 86
Robotnik (The Worker), 69, 103, 107
Rokosowski, Konstantin, 27, 30
Roman Catholic Church, 12, 33, 35, 42
Rome, 87, 119
Roosevelt, Franklin D., 26
Rulewski, Jan, 78, 123, 125
Russia, Czarist, 13–15
Russian revolutionary movement, 15
Rzeszow, 73
Rural Solidarity, 38, 77, 78

St. Stanislaw, 37
St. Zbawicieka, 33
Samsonowicz, Henryk, 68, 79
Saxony, 14
Schleswig Holstein, 97
Sejm, 13, 14, 16, 30
Self-controlled revolution, 77
Self-governing trade, 113
Self-government, 35, 77
Sigismund, 11, 14
Sigismund's Column, 26
Sikorski, General Wladyslaw, 20, 21, 23
Silesia, 26, 56, 101
Slowik, Kazimierz, 67
Socialism, 15, 110
Sojuz 81, 74, 81, 85
Soviet Communist Party, 12
Soviet intervention, 84
Spanish Civil War, 22
Spychalski, Marshal, 38
Stalin, Josef, 19–22, 26, 27, 28
Stalinism, 27, 29, 33, 48
Strewicz, Artur, 30
Sweden, 14
Szczecin, 44, 60, 65, 101
Szczepanski, Maciej, 65

Tarnowska, Countess, 24
Third Reich, 32
Tito, Josip Broz, 27
TKN (mobile underground teaching insti-
   tute), 68
Turks, 15
Twentieth Party Congress, 28
Treaty of Versailles, 16

Ukraine, 18
Unita, 79
United Peasants Alliance, 30, 78
United States, 16, 57, 81
Ursus Factory, 41, 42, 49, 52, 67, 69, 75, 94
U.S. Air Force, 85
U.S.S.R., 9, 18, 19, 21, 22, 26, 30, 32, 42,
   70, 82, 85, 98
Ustrzyki Dolme, 75

Vatican, 37, 46
Vienna, 15

Vistula, 23, 94
Vladimir the Great, 13
Voievodas (prefects), 84
Voyvodship party, 37
von Seeckt, General, 15

Walbrzych, 94
Walesa, Anna, 103
Walesa, Bogdan, 102
Walesa, Jaroslaw, 102
Walesa, Miroslawa (Danuta), 99, 101, 102,
   114, 116, 118
Walesa, Przemyslaw, 102
Walesa, Slawomir, 102
Walesa, Stanislaw, 118
Walentynowicz, Anna, 52, 53, 88, 89, 90,
   103, 104, 118
Warsaw, 8, 10, 16, 18, 21, 23, 24, 26–85 pas-
   sim, 27, 30, 33, 84, 94–122 passim
Warsaw Pact, 9, 40, 41, 71, 82, 85
Warsaw Rising, 23
Warsaw University, 35, 42, 68, 71, 79
Western Allies, 20
Western-style parliament, 110
Westernization, 13
Washington, 84
White House, 84, 87
Wiez, 68
Wilson, Woodrow, 16
Wladislaw I, 13
Wloclawek, 73
Wojtyla, Cardinal Karol, see John Paul II
World War I, 15, 18
World War II, 12, 19, 23, 24, 32, 96, 98
Workers' consciousness, 104
Workers' council, 16
Wroclaw, 30, 46, 67
Wyszynski, Cardinal Stefan, 36, 37, 38, 39,
   42, 43, 46, 65, 118, 119

Yalta, 24, 26

Zamosc, 84
Zawadski, 30
Zeran, 49
Zieja, Father, 68
Zionism, 35
Zrem, 104